On Free Choice
of the Will

AUGUSTINE

On Free Choice
of the Will

Translated by
Thomas Williams

Hackett Publishing Company
Indianapolis / Cambridge

Augustine: 354–430

Copyright © 1993 by Hackett Publishing Company, Inc.

14 13 12 11 10   6 7 8 9 10

Cover design by Listenberger & Associates
Interior design by Dan Kirklin

For further information, please address

Hackett Publishing Company, Inc.
P.O. Box 44937
Indianapolis, Indiana 46244-0937

www.hackettpublishing.com

Library of Congress Cataloging-in-Publication Data

Augustine, Saint, Bishop of Hippo.
    [De libero arbitrio. English]
    On free choice of the will/Augustine; translated, with introduction
and notes, by Thomas Williams.
            p.   cm.
    Includes bibliographical references.
    ISBN 0-87220-189-9 (cloth)   ISBN 0-87220-188-0 (pbk.)
    1. Free will and determinism—Early works to 1800. 2. God—
Omnipotence—Early works to 1800. I. Williams, Thomas, 1967–
II. Title.
BR65.A664E5   1993
233'.7—dc20   93-22170
                                                          CIP

ISBN-13: 978-0-87220-189-7 (cloth)
ISBN-13: 978-0-87220-188-0 (pbk.)

For My Parents

Contents

Note on the Translation

My aim in this translation has been to reproduce as faithfully as possible Augustine's meaning, emphasis, and sequence of thought. I have made no attempt to reproduce the polysyllabic splendor of Augustine's Latin; such weighty rhetoric is too much for the slender skeleton of contemporary English to bear. This decision has frequently meant sacrificing some of Augustine's favorite rhetorical devices: for example, his habit of expressing arguments in the negative, and often in interrogative form; his tendency to apologize for metaphors by inserting an expression like "as it were" or "in a certain sense"; and his repetitions for rhetorical effect. In choosing between a literal but turgid translation and a freer but crisper one, I have preferred the latter, provided always that the meaning and emphasis are preserved.

I have adopted gender-inclusive language only where it could be used without calling attention to itself. It would be the worst of anachronisms to make Augustine sound as if he had the same concerns about inclusiveness that we have nowadays. In general, I have preferred 'human being' to 'man' in the generic sense. Where appropriate, I have also changed singular subjects to plural in order to allow the use of common-gender pronouns. Otherwise my usage is that of traditional English, in which the masculine bias is actually less pronounced than it is in Latin.

References to Scripture are given in accordance with the verse and chapter divisions of the New Revised Standard Version of the Bible.

For the Latin text of *On Free Choice of the Will* I used the critical edition in the *Corpus Christianorum: Series Latina*, volume 29, edited by W. M. Green (Turnhout, Belgium: Brepols, 1970). Except for its surprisingly frequent typographical errors, this edition is the same as the one that appeared earlier in the *Corpus Scriptorum Ecclesiasticorum Latinorum*. I have adopted variant readings in two places: at page 256, line 22, for 'iuste videndum est' read 'iuste vivendum est'; and at page 276, line 6, for 'bonum hominem' read 'primum hominem'. In addition, at page 308, line 47, I have emended 'esse' to 'esset'.

For the Latin text of the *Reconsiderations* I used the critical edition from the same series, volume 57, edited by Almut Mutzenbecher

(1984). It should be noted that the quotations that appear in the
Reconsiderations do not always correspond word for word with
the text that appears in *On Free Choice of the Will.*

I wish to thank Professor Alfred J. Freddoso of the University
of Notre Dame, without whose encouragement I would not have
undertaken this translation. And I am especially grateful to Professor Paul Spade of Indiana University, who read the entire translation with painstaking care and great insight. To him I owe the
elimination of any number of errors and infelicities, and many
helpful suggestions for improvement.

Introduction

Despite its relative brevity, *On Free Choice of the Will* contains almost every distinctive feature of Augustine's philosophy. It presents the essentials of his ethics, his theory of knowledge, and his views of God and human nature. It is therefore the ideal introduction to Augustine's thought for introductory courses and surveys of medieval philosophy, where there is not time for a complete and detailed reading of longer works such as the *Confessions* and *The City of God*. But its very richness makes it impossible for me to discuss in this brief introduction even all of the more important aspects of this work. In what follows, therefore, I concern myself chiefly with the two concepts that figure in the title: *freedom* and *the will*.

The word 'freedom' has many senses. One sort of freedom involves the absence of restraints. As long as the door is not locked, I am *free* (in this sense) to leave the room. We might call this *physical* freedom. Physical freedom means that there is nothing to hinder me from acting as I choose to act.

But suppose I live in a deterministic universe. Every choice I make is determined by prior states of the universe, states over which I have no control. I may still be physically free—no one has locked me up or tied me down—but it seems that I lack freedom in some stronger and more interesting sense. I am free to act as I choose, but my choices themselves are not free. The freedom to choose in a way that is not determined by anything outside my control is what I shall call *metaphysical* freedom.

The view that human beings have metaphysical freedom is called 'libertarianism'. Libertarianism is no longer a popular view among philosophers, most of whom think that at best we have only physical freedom. But Augustine was one of the great defenders of libertarianism; indeed, he was the first to articulate the view clearly. According to Augustine, human beings are endowed with a power that he calls the will. Augustine compares the will to the weight of an inanimate object. Just as a falling apple is carried to the ground by its weight, so a human being is carried to his goal (whatever that may be) by his will. But the analogy is deficient in one important respect. The falling apple has no say about where its weight will take it. A human being,

however, can use his will to go in a seemingly limitless variety
of directions. This feature of the will Augustine calls *liberum arbi-
trium*, which can be translated as "freedom of decision" or (more
usually) "free choice." Because it has free choice, the will, truly
the captain of its soul, looks out over the vast sea of good things
and sails wherever it pleases, blithely unaffected by the winds
and waves of cause and effect that steer unthinking and unfree
vessels. Thus, the will is not determined by any external factors.
Only the will can determine itself to choose. This freedom is what
allows us to be responsible for our actions; if outside forces beyond
our control caused us to choose to act in a certain way, we could
hardly be held responsible for acting in that way.

Thus far I have talked about being determined by *external*
things. Some philosophers would object to this as an unfair charac-
terization of their views. "We agree," they might say, "that if
our choices are caused by external forces, then they are not our
responsibility. But it is not external states that determine our
choices; it is *internal* states: beliefs, desires, states of character,
and so on. And since it is *my* desires and *my* character that determine *my* choices, my freedom is not threatened."

A libertarian like Augustine would not be convinced by this
sort of reasoning. These philosophers still insist that my choices
are determined; the fact that they are determined by internal
rather than external factors is inconsequential. It is no better to
be a hand puppet than a marionette. Besides, to a libertarian, this
view is just a dodge. To see why this is the case, suppose that I
have made some choice that was determined by my state of
character at the time of the choice. Call that state of character S.
How did I acquire S? If we admit that determinism is true, we
must say that, given the laws of nature and the causal factors at
work both inside and outside me, S is the inevitable result of
some prior state R. And how did I acquire R? It was the result
of some prior state Q, which in turn was the result of some prior
state P, and so on. And thus we trace the causal chain back in
time, eventually reaching a point before I was born. But how can
I be responsible for choices that are the assured causal results of
states of the universe that existed before I was born? For obviously
I have no control over things that happened before I was born.
The fact that this causal chain eventually wormed its way inside
me, so to speak, determining my choices from within, no longer

seems to guarantee my freedom. It is with such considerations in mind that Augustine rejects the view (known as 'compatibilism') that determinism is compatible with human freedom and moral responsibility; and since he is convinced that human beings are in fact free and responsible, he must reject determinism as well.

Because human beings have metaphysical freedom, we are capable of making a real difference in the world. We do not merely play the parts that the laws of nature and the past history of the universe have written for us; to some extent at least, we write our own scripts. In this way we can truly be said to be in the image of God, who created all things distinct from himself by a free and unconditioned act of the will. Like God, human beings can introduce genuine change, can bring into being something that except for their free choice would never have existed.

Unfortunately, this metaphysical freedom can be used— indeed, Augustine thinks that it *has* been used—to introduce evil into the world. The initial problem for Augustine in *On Free Choice of the Will* is whether God is the cause of this evil. Suppose there is no metaphysical freedom. Then any evil that exists would be the inevitable and predictable result of the initial conditions of the universe (the state it was in at the very beginning) and the laws of nature (which are just the rules that the universe follows in going from one state to the next). And it would be plausible to assign responsibility for that evil to whoever set up the initial conditions and the laws of nature. But of course that was God. And so Evodius asks at the beginning of Book One, "Isn't God the cause of evil?"

Augustine's answer is that human beings have metaphysical freedom, and so the blame for any evil action rests on the person who performed that action. But then one might object, "If metaphysical freedom can lead to evil, then shouldn't God be blamed for giving it to us in the first place?" Augustine agrees that without metaphysical freedom there would be no evil, but he also thinks that there would be no genuine good either. Without metaphysical freedom, the universe is just a divine puppet show. If there is to be any real creaturely goodness, any new and creative act of love, rather than the merely mechanical uncoiling of a wind-up universe, if there are to be any real decisions other than those made in the divine will, then there must be metaphysical freedom, and such freedom brings with it the possibility of evil as well as the promise of goodness.

There is a third sense of 'freedom' that I shall call *autonomy*. Augustine describes autonomy as "the sort of freedom that people have in mind when they think they are free because they have no human masters, or that people desire when they want to be set free by their masters." This sort of freedom is not freedom in the highest and most genuine sense, Augustine believes, and so he has little to say about it. For our present purposes, however, the very fact that Augustine regards it as unimportant is itself an important part of his view. For many later philosophers have thought that autonomy is crucially important. As a moral (rather than a political or social) concept, autonomy is a cornerstone of the very influential views of the eighteenth-century philosopher Immanuel Kant. According to Kant, morality requires that the agent be completely autonomous. To be a grown-up, morally speaking, means being your own boss. It means giving yourself the law by which you govern your actions, rather than accepting that law from other people or from your desires.

Augustine, however, would point out that if you are your own boss, you are *ipso facto* your own slave. And it is not right to be ruled by what is equal to oneself. One should be ruled only by what is in every respect superior to oneself, and that is Truth, which Augustine identifies with God. The unchanging divine truth about what we ought to do is what Augustine calls the eternal law. The morally grown-up human being recognizes this law for what it is: an immutable standard of divine authority, one that binds us unconditionally, quite independently of what we may happen to desire or believe.

The Kantian doctrine has an undeniable appeal, but Augustine would point out that evil always has a specious attractiveness and that error is most dangerous when it is parasitic on some truth. The truth in this case is that moral adulthood requires that we *see* the law for ourselves. That is what Augustine means by saying that we must try to understand what we have already believed. Children must be taught by others what is right, but mature human beings seek to understand it for themselves, no longer relying on what they have heard from others. The error is to think that because we must *see* it for ourselves, we must also *make* it for ourselves. If I *make* my own laws, I can also *change* my own laws. If I *bind* myself, I can also *release* myself. If I think that the moral law has no higher authority than my own reason, I can easily come to think that it has no real authority at all.[1]

Augustine, by contrast, insists on the absolute objectivity and authority of the eternal law. Those who taught me about that law were not making that law for me, any more than Isaac Newton made the law of gravity. In either case, the teacher was merely articulating something that was already there. Someone who tries to violate the law of gravity is not committing a personal affront against Isaac Newton: he is thumbing his nose at the very fabric of the universe, and the consequence will be tremendous physical pain. Similarly, someone who runs afoul of the law of morality is not simply offending his teachers: he is violating the fundamental order of the universe, and the consequence will be tremendous moral pain, which Augustine describes quite effectively in chapter 11 of Book One:

> Fear attacks from one side and desire from the other; from one side, anxiety; from the other, an empty and deceptive happiness; from one side, the agony of losing what one loved; from the other, the passion to acquire what one did not have; from one side, the pain of an injury received; from the other, the burning desire to avenge it. Wherever you turn, avarice can pinch, extravagance squander, ambition destroy, pride swell, envy torment, apathy crush, obstinacy incite, oppression chafe, and countless other evils crowd the realm of inordinate desire and run riot.

This is not the arbitrary judgment of a killjoy God; it is the natural and inevitable result of trying to live in a law-governed universe while defying its laws.

This is one reason why Augustine thinks that it is important to understand what we have believed. So long as we rely on other people for our moral beliefs, we are in danger of coming to think that morality is merely a matter of other people's opinions—or of our own opinions, for that matter. Even if we evade that danger, our confidence in our moral beliefs will never exceed our confi-

---

1. I by no means wish to suggest that Kant himself fell into this way of thinking about the moral law, for he did not. I mean only to say that this element of Kant's thought can easily lead one in this direction.

dence in our teachers. And everyone knows that even the best teacher is fallible, especially in the realm of morality, where human beings are all too apt to invest a personal preference with all the dignity of a universal precept, or (worse yet) to treat a universal precept as if it were just a matter of taste.

Our only security against this instability of moral belief is to attain understanding or knowledge, rather then mere belief, about moral matters. Augustine's distinction between belief (or faith) and knowledge is an unusual one. He often makes this distinction by using an analogy from sensation. "Faith comes by hearing,"[2] but knowledge comes by sight. Never having been to Memphis, Egypt, I do not *know* that there is such a place. I merely *believe* that such a place exists because I have *heard* about it from reliable sources. By contrast, I have *seen* Memphis, Tennessee, so I *know* that it exists.

This distinction holds not only for the objects of physical sensation (what Augustine calls "sensible things"), but also for the objects of intellectual understanding ("intelligible things"). If someone asks me what is the sum of 2 and 2, I can say that I *know* it is 4. I can just *see* that $2 + 2 = 4$. But I do not have the mathematical training to *see* the truth of some highly complicated theorem; if I have any opinion at all about such a theorem, it can only be belief, not knowledge. I must take some mathematician's word for it.

When it comes to moral truths, which are a special sub-class of intelligible things, it is not quite so clear what sort of training or intellectual skills one needs in order to attain knowledge— that is, to see for oneself what is right and good. One thing is certain, however. Augustine is convinced that "Unless you believe, you will not understand."[3] Unless you have already come to have certain moral beliefs on the basis of what you have heard from your parents or teachers, you will never be in a position to see for yourself that these beliefs are true, and thus to attain moral knowledge. This may sound like arguing in a circle, or at least like a kind of prooftexting ("Here's what I believe; now I'll try to prove that I'm right"), but in fact it is a very plausible position.

2. Romans 10:17
3. Isaiah 7:9 (pre-Vulgate text)

If you are brought up among people who believe that physicists are deceitful tools of an imperialistic conspiracy trying to dupe an unwitting public, you are likely to come to share that belief. As a result, it is highly improbable that you will ever take the trouble to study physics and thus come to see that physics tells us a lot of true and interesting things about the sensible world. If a physicist ever tries to demonstrate to you the truth of one of his claims, you will respond to his arguments, however cogent they may be, by shrugging your shoulders and saying "You only say that because you're a physicist." And yet (and this is the important point) the physicist will still be right, and your disbelief is utterly irrelevant to that. The law of gravity will not cease to operate simply because you are skeptical of physicists; even if everyone on earth lost all confidence in natural science, we would not thereby achieve weightlessness.

Moral truths are no different. Belief is required for understanding. If you are brought up among people who think that morality is just a matter of opinion, it is highly improbable that you will ever be able to see that moralists teach us a lot of true and interesting things about the intelligible world. If someone ever tries to demonstrate to you that some moral belief is true, you will respond by saying "You only say that because you're a moralist." And yet the moralist will still be right, and your disbelief is utterly irrelevant to that. The law against murder is not abrogated simply because you are a relativist; even if every human being repudiated belief in objective moral standards, murder would not cease to be wrong. So belief is necessary for the attainment of knowledge, but belief is incomplete and unstable until it is replaced by knowledge. All of Augustine's philosophical writing may be seen as an attempt first to awaken belief and then to raise it to the level of knowledge.

A strict understanding of moral autonomy, then, is for Augustine a mere error. Where human beings are concerned, there is no such thing as being free from a law that is imposed from without; to deny the authority of the eternal law is not moral adulthood but moral perversity. Moral uprightness, therefore, consists in submission to this eternal and immutable truth, which is not of our own making.

So much we can easily understand. But why does Augustine go on to say that not merely moral uprightness, but *freedom*, consists in submission to the Truth? Even if we give up the notion of autonomy, it seems rather peculiar to say that *submission* to anything can bring us *freedom*.

This brings us to the final sense of freedom. Since Augustine thinks of this sort of freedom as the highest and most valuable sort, I shall call it *genuine* freedom. Genuine freedom involves using one's metaphysical freedom to cleave to the eternal law, to love what is good, to submit to the truth. Augustine has two main arguments for the claim that submission to the truth is the only genuine freedom. The first is given explicitly in chapters 13 and 14 of Book Two. The soul enjoys nothing with freedom unless it enjoys it securely. But truth and goodness are the only things that cannot be taken from the soul against its will. So the soul that submits to the truth and loves the good will be free, while the soul that is fixed on lesser things is at the mercy of forces beyond its control.

The second argument is given implicitly in the rest of Book Two and the first half of Book Three. In these chapters Augustine explains his view of the relationship between being and goodness, a view that has deep roots in Plato and later becomes the common property of medieval Christian thinkers. A quick overview of this discussion is needed before we can see how it bears on the nature of genuine freedom.

Everything that exists is characterized by some degree of order, number, and measure; or in other terminology, every nature has form. A nature is good to the extent that it has form, that is, to the extent that it lives up to the standards of order, number, and measure that are characteristic of that nature. For example, it is characteristic of knives to cut, so a good knife is one that cuts well.

So the more form a nature has, the more goodness it has; and it is also true that the more form a nature has, the more being it has. Augustine therefore claims that everything is good insofar as it exists. For to the extent that something lacks goodness, it lacks being, and if something comes to lack goodness altogether, it simply passes out of existence. Evil, as Augustine understands it, is a mere deficiency. It is not a positive reality, a nature; it is a privation of form, a blot on the order, number, and measure of some nature.

Every nature, then, comes from God, who is the source of all being and goodness, and everything that exists is good insofar as it exists. Even in the act of condemning something we acknowledge this fact. For unless we acknowledged that a nature was good, we would not condemn a deficiency in that nature; we would not think of that deficiency as evil, as a regrettable blemish on the beautiful face of being. "What justly displeases you in the flaw is that it spoils what pleases you in the nature."

Because human beings come from God, who *is* in the highest degree, they love existence. That is to say, the fundamental human desire is to *be* in the fullest possible sense. But as we have seen, to be means to have a nature. So the only ultimately satisfying thing for human beings is to live up to their nature. When the will turns away from the highest good to lower goods, it frustrates the very law of its nature, putting what is inferior above what is superior, subjecting itself to the things it ought to master. The only genuine freedom, then, is submission to the truth. In other words, obedience to the eternal law, which is no arbitrary divine pronouncement but the rules for action that are stamped on our very nature, is our only security against frustration, dissatisfaction, confusion, and the tyranny of bad habits and misplaced priorities.

As Augustine understands it, violating the eternal law is not like doing 40 in a 35-mile-per-hour zone when there is no traffic around; it is more like trying to violate the law of gravity. But note once again the crucial difference. An apple falling from a tree has no choice about whether to obey the law of gravity. It has no option to frustrate its own nature. But since the will is free, it has a choice about whether to obey the eternal law. Human beings can voluntarily wreck their lives by running afoul of the laws that govern their nature. This is indeed a sort of freedom, but it can hardly be the best sort. That very will by which human beings fight against the law of their own nature, a law that they did not make and from which they cannot escape, can be used to love that law and live up to that nature. A soul that has such a will is genuinely free: free from a hopeless struggle against itself, free to become what it most truly is.

Selected Bibliography

Other Important Works by Augustine

City of God. Translated by Henry Bettenson. Introduced by John O'Meara. New York: Penguin Books, 1984.

Confessions. Translated by F. J. Sheed. Introduced by Peter Brown. Indianapolis and Cambridge: Hackett Publishing Company, 1993.

The Trinity. Translated by Edmund Hill. Brooklyn: New City Press, 1990.

Works about Augustine

A Companion to the Study of St. Augustine. Edited by Roy W. Battenhouse. Grand Rapids: Baker Book House, 1979. Contains an especially helpful essay on Augustine's view of the relationship between faith and reason.

Augustine of Hippo. A biography by Peter Brown. Berkeley and Los Angeles: University of California Press, 1967. Widely regarded as the best biography of Augustine.

The Christian Philosophy of St. Augustine. Etienne Gilson, translated by L.E.M. Lynch. New York: Octagon Books, 1988. The best general introduction to Augustine. Although sometimes inaccurate in its presentation of the details of Augustine's thought, it captures the spirit of his thinking.

Guide to the Study of Saint Augustine. Eugène Portalié, translated by Ralph J. Bastian, introduction by Vernon J. Bourke. London: Burns & Oates, 1960. A useful corrective to some of Gilson's mistakes, especially regarding the doctrine of illumination. Generally accurate as to details, at least on the purely philosophical issues, but completely missing the spirit of Augustine's thought.

Wisdom from St. Augustine. Vernon J. Bourke. Houston: Center for Thomistic Studies, 1984. The essay "Moral Illumination" is a helpful study of some of the issues raised in *On Free Choice of the Will.*

On Free Choice
of the Will

Book One

1.

EVODIUS: Please tell me: isn't God the cause of evil?

AUGUSTINE: I will tell you once you have made clear what kind of evil you are asking about. For we use the word 'evil' in two senses: first, when we say that someone has *done* evil; and second, when we say that someone has *suffered* evil.

EVODIUS: I want to know about both.

AUGUSTINE: But if you know or believe that God is good—and it is not right to believe otherwise—then he does no evil. On the other hand, if we acknowledge that God is just—and it is impious to deny it—then he rewards the good and punishes the wicked. Those punishments are certainly evils for those who suffer them. Therefore, if no one is punished unjustly—and we must believe this, since we believe that this universe is governed by divine providence—it follows that God is a cause of the second kind of evil, but in no way causes the first kind.

EVODIUS: Then is there some other cause of the evil that God does not cause?

AUGUSTINE: There certainly is. Such evil could not occur unless someone caused it. But if you ask who that someone is, it is impossible to say. For there is no single cause of evil; rather, everyone who does evil is the cause of his own evildoing. If you doubt this, recall what I said earlier: Evil deeds are punished by the justice of God. They would not be punished justly if they had not been performed voluntarily.

EVODIUS: It seems that no one could sin unless he had first learned how to sin. And if that is the case, I must ask this: From whom did we learn to sin?

AUGUSTINE: Do you think learning is a good thing?

EVODIUS: Who would dare to say that learning is a bad thing?

AUGUSTINE: What if it is neither good nor bad?

EVODIUS: I think it is good.

AUGUSTINE: Indeed it is, since knowledge is given or awakened through learning, and no one comes to know anything except through learning.[1] Don't you agree?

---

1. In the passage that follows, Augustine relies on the similarity between the verb *'discere'* ('to learn') and its noun form *'disciplina'* ('learning').

EVODIUS: I think that we come to know only good things through learning.

AUGUSTINE: Then we do not come to know evil things; for the word 'learning' is correctly applied only when we come to know something.[2]

EVODIUS: But if we do not come to know evil things, how is it that human beings perform evil acts?

AUGUSTINE: Perhaps because they turn away from learning and become strangers to it. But whether that is the correct explanation or not, one thing is certainly clear: since learning is good, and the word 'learning' is correctly applied only when we come to know something, we simply cannot come to know evil things. If we could, then they would be part of learning, and so learning would not be a good thing. But it *is* a good thing, as you said yourself. Therefore, we do not come to know evil things, and there is no point in your asking from whom we learn to do evil things. Or else we do come to know them, but only as things to be avoided, not as things to be done. It follows that doing evil is nothing but turning away from learning.

EVODIUS: I rather think that there are two sorts of learning: one by means of which we learn to do right, and another by means of which we learn to do evil. But when you asked whether learning was good, the love of good itself caught my attention, and I saw only the sort of learning by which we learn to do right. That is why I answered that it is good. But now I remember that there is another sort of learning. I have no doubt that it is evil, and I would like to know its cause.

AUGUSTINE: Do you at least consider understanding good?

EVODIUS: Certainly. I consider it so good that I cannot see how any human trait could be better. And I would in no way say that any understanding can be bad.

AUGUSTINE: When someone is being taught but does not understand, would you think that he has learned?

Unfortunately, the words are so similar in English that a literal translation sounds odd and occasionally nonsensical. I have therefore translated '*discere*' as 'come to know' in most cases. The reader should bear in mind that the connection between 'come to know' and 'learning' is much closer in the Latin than I can safely make it in the English.

2. Literally, "the word '*disciplina*' is derived from the word '*discere*'."

EVODIUS: Of course not.

AUGUSTINE: Well then, if all understanding is good, and no one who does not understand learns, then everyone who learns is doing good. For everyone who learns, understands; and everyone who understands is doing good. So someone who wants to know the cause of our learning something really wants to know the cause of our doing good. So let's have no more of your wanting to hunt down this mysterious evil teacher. If he is evil, he is no teacher; and if he is a teacher, he is not evil.

EVODIUS: Now that you have convinced me that we do not learn **2.** to do evil, please explain to me what *is* the source of our evildoing.

AUGUSTINE: You have hit upon the very question that worried me greatly when I was still young, a question that wore me out, drove me into the company of heretics,[3] and knocked me flat on my face. I was so hurt by this fall, buried under a mountain of silly fairy tales, that if my love of finding the truth had not secured divine help, I would not have been able to get out from under them to breathe freely and begin to seek the truth. And since such pains were taken to free me from this difficulty, I will lead you on the same path that I followed in making my escape. God will be with us, and he will make us understand what we have believed. For we are well aware that we are at the stage described by the prophet, who says, "Unless you believe, you will not understand."[4] We believe that everything that exists comes from the one God, and yet we believe that God is not the cause of sins. What is troubling is that if you admit that sins come from the souls that God created, and those souls come from God, pretty soon you'll be tracing those sins back to God.

EVODIUS: You have stated plainly what bothers me in thinking about this question. That is the problem that has compelled me and drawn me into this inquiry.

AUGUSTINE: Be courageous, and go on believing what you believe. There is no better belief, even if you do not yet see the explanation for why it is true. The truest beginning of piety is to think as highly of God as possible; and doing so means that one must

---

3. The Manichees, who believed in the existence of an evil "god" equal to and independent of the good "god"

4. Isaiah 7:9 (pre-Vulgate text)

believe that he is omnipotent, and not changeable in the smallest respect; that he is the creator of all good things, but is himself more excellent than all of them; that he is the supremely just ruler of everything that he created; and that he was not aided in creating by any other being, as if he were not sufficiently powerful by himself. It follows that he created all things from nothing. He did not create from himself, but generated one who is equal to himself, whom we call the only Son of God. In trying to describe the Son more clearly we call him "the Power of God and the Wisdom of God,"[5] through whom God made all the things that were made from nothing. On that basis let us try, with God's help, to achieve an understanding of the problem you have raised.

3.   You want to know the source of our evildoing. So we must first discuss what evildoing *is*. State your view on the matter. If you cannot explain the whole thing at once in a few words, you can at least show me your view by naming particular evil deeds.

EVODIUS: Adultery, murder, and sacrilege, not to mention others that time and memory do not permit me to enumerate. Who could fail to recognize these as evil deeds?

AUGUSTINE: Tell me first, why do you think adultery is evil? Because the law forbids it?

EVODIUS: On the contrary. Clearly, it is not evil because the law forbids it; rather, the law forbids it because it is evil.

AUGUSTINE: But suppose someone were to make things difficult for us by extolling the pleasures of adultery and asking why we think adultery evil and deserving of condemnation. Surely you do not think that people who want to understand, and not merely to believe, would have to take refuge in an appeal to the authority of the law? Now like you I do believe, and believe most firmly, and cry out that all peoples and nations should believe, that adultery is evil. But now we are attempting to know and hold firmly by understanding what we have already accepted by faith. So think this over as carefully as you can, and tell me what reason you have by which you know that adultery is evil.

EVODIUS: I know that it is evil because I would not tolerate it if someone tried to commit adultery with my own wife. Anyone who does to another what he does not want done to himself does evil.

5. 1 Corinthians 1:24

AUGUSTINE: What if someone's lust is so great that he offers his wife to another and willingly allows him to commit adultery with her, and is eager to enjoy the same freedom with the other man's wife? Do you think that this man has done nothing evil?
EVODIUS: Far from it!
AUGUSTINE: But by your rule he does not sin, since he is not doing anything that he is unwilling to have done to himself. You must therefore look for some other argument to show that adultery is evil.
EVODIUS: The reason that I think it is evil is that I have often seen people condemned for this crime.
AUGUSTINE: But haven't people often been condemned for good deeds? Not to refer you to any other books, recall the story that is superior to all others by virtue of its divine authority. There you will find that we must think very poorly of the apostles and martyrs if we intend to make condemnation a sure sign of wrongdoing. All of them were judged worthy of condemnation because of their confession of faith. It follows that if everything that is condemned is evil, it was evil in those days to believe in Christ and to confess that faith. But if not everything that is condemned is evil, find some other way to show why adultery is evil.
EVODIUS: I can't think how to respond.
AUGUSTINE: Then perhaps what makes adultery evil is inordinate desire,[6] whereas so long as you look for the evil in the external, visible act, you are bound to encounter difficulties. In order to

---

6. The Latin here is *'libido'*. There is no single English word that adequately conveys its meaning. Some translators have rendered it 'desire', with the result that Augustine often seems to be saying that all desire is sinful, which is not his view at all. The alternative translation of 'lust' captures the fact that *'libido'* is one specific kind of desire, but English usage restricts 'lust' to blameworthy *sexual* desire; and Augustine certainly does not mean to claim that all murder and sacrilege result from misdirected sexual passion. Therefore, despite the occasional clumsiness of doing so, I have translated *'libido'* as 'inordinate desire'. The other important term in this passage is *'cupiditas'*. Sometimes Augustine treats *'cupiditas'* as synonymous with *'libido'*; in those cases I have translated it as 'cupidity'. But sometimes he uses it as a neutral term, and there I have translated it as 'desire'.

understand that inordinate desire is what makes adultery evil, consider this: if a man is unable to sleep with someone else's wife, but it is somehow clear that he would like to, and would do so if he had the chance, he is no less guilty than if he were caught in the act.

EVODIUS: Nothing could be clearer. Now I see that there is no need for a long discussion to persuade me that this is the case with murder and sacrilege and every sin whatsoever. For it is clear now that inordinate desire is what drives every kind of evildoing.

4. AUGUSTINE: Do you know that inordinate desire is also called 'cupidity'?

EVODIUS: Yes.

AUGUSTINE: Do you think there is any difference between cupidity and fear? Or are they quite the same?

EVODIUS: Indeed, I think there is a huge difference between the two.

AUGUSTINE: I suppose you think so because cupidity desires its object, and fear flees from it.

EVODIUS: You're quite right.

AUGUSTINE: Then suppose a man kills someone, not out of cupidity for something that he desires to gain, but because he fears that some harm will come to himself. Would he be a murderer?

EVODIUS: Yes, he would. But even in this deed, cupidity is the driving force: for a man who kills someone out of fear surely desires to live without fear.

AUGUSTINE: Do you think that living without fear is a small good?

EVODIUS: It is a great good, but that murderer cannot achieve it by his action.

AUGUSTINE: I am not asking what he can achieve, but what he desires. Someone who desires a life free from fear certainly desires a good thing, so his desire is not blameworthy; otherwise we will have to blame everyone who loves the good. Consequently, we will have to say that there is an instance of murder in which cupidity is not the driving force; and it will be false that inordinate desire is what drives all sins, to the extent that they are evil. Either that, or there will be an instance of murder that is not sinful.

EVODIUS: If murder is just killing a human being, then there can be murder that is not sinful. When a soldier kills the enemy, when a judge or his representative puts a criminal to death, or when a weapon accidentally slips out of someone's hand without his willing or noticing it: these people do not seem to me to be sinning when they kill someone.

AUGUSTINE: I agree, but such people are not usually called murderers. So consider someone who kills his master because he fears severe torture. Do you think that he should be classed among those who kill a human being but do not deserve to be called murderers?

EVODIUS: I think this case is entirely different. In the earlier examples, those men are acting in accordance with the law, or at least not contrary to the law; but no law approves of the deed in your example.

AUGUSTINE: Again you refer me to authority. You must remember that we took up this discussion in order to understand what we believe. We believe the laws, and so we must try to understand, if we can, whether the law that punishes this deed does so unjustly.

EVODIUS: It is in no way unjust to punish someone who knowingly and willingly kills his master. None of the men in my earlier examples did that.

AUGUSTINE: But do you not remember that a little while ago you said that inordinate desire is what drives every evil deed, and that this is the very reason why the deed is evil?

EVODIUS: Of course I remember.

AUGUSTINE: And did you not also grant that someone who desires to live without fear does not have an evil desire?

EVODIUS: I remember that too.

AUGUSTINE: It follows that, since the master is killed by the slave as a result of this desire, he is not killed as a result of a blameworthy desire. And so we have not yet figured out why this deed is evil. For we are agreed that all wrongdoing is evil only because it results from inordinate desire, that is, from blameworthy cupidity.

EVODIUS: At this point it seems to me that the slave is unjustly condemned, which I would not dream of saying if I could think of some other response.

AUGUSTINE: You have let yourself be persuaded that this great crime should go unpunished, without considering whether the slave wanted to be free of the fear of his master in order to satisfy his own inordinate desires. All wicked people, just like good people, desire to live without fear. The difference is that the good, in desiring this, turn their love away from things that cannot be possessed without the fear of losing them. The wicked, on the other hand, try to get rid of anything that prevents them from enjoying such things securely. Thus they lead a wicked and criminal life, which would better be called death.

EVODIUS: Now I've come to my senses. I am glad that I understand so clearly the nature of that blameworthy cupidity that is called inordinate desire. Obviously it is the love of those things that one can lose against one's will.

5.   So, if you don't mind, why don't we go on to consider whether inordinate desire is also the driving force in acts of sacrilege, most of which, as we see, are committed out of superstition?

AUGUSTINE: I think you're being too hasty. First, I think, we should discuss whether an attacking enemy or an ambushing murderer can be killed without any inordinate desire, for the sake of preserving one's life, liberty, or chastity.

EVODIUS: How can I think that people are without inordinate desire when they fight fiercely for things that they can lose against their will? Or if those things cannot be lost, what need is there to resort to killing for their sake?

AUGUSTINE: Then the law is unjust that permits a traveler to kill a highway robber in order to keep from being killed himself, or that permits anyone who can, man or woman, to kill a sexual assailant, before he or she is harmed. The law also commands a soldier to kill the enemy; and if he refuses, he is subject to penalties from his commander. Surely we will not dare to say that these laws are unjust, or rather, that they are not laws at all. For it seems to me that an unjust law is no law at all.

EVODIUS: I see that the law is quite secure against this sort of objection, for it permits lesser evils among the people that it governs in order to prevent greater evils. It is much better that one who plots against another's life should be killed rather than one who is defending his own life. And it is much worse for someone unwillingly to suffer a sexual assault, than for the assailant to be killed by the one he was going to assault. A soldier who kills the enemy is acting as an agent of the law, so he can easily perform his duty without inordinate desire. Furthermore, the law itself, which was established with a view to protecting the people, cannot be accused of any inordinate desire. As for the one who enacted the law, if he did so at God's command—that is, if he did what eternal justice prescribes—he could do so without any inordinate desire at all. But even if he did act out of inordinate desire, it does not follow that one must be guilty of inordinate desire in obeying the law; for a good law can be enacted by one who is not himself good. For example, suppose that someone who had gained tyrannical power accepted a bribe from some interested party to make it illegal to take a woman by force, even for marriage. The law would not be bad merely in virtue of the fact that the one who made it was unjust and corrupt. Therefore, the law that commands that enemy forces be repulsed by an equal force for the protection of the citizens can be obeyed without inordinate desire. The same can be said of all officials who by lawful order are subject to some higher power.

But as for those other men, I do not see how they can be excused, even if the law itself is just. For the law does not force them to kill; it merely leaves that in their power. They are free not to kill anyone for those things which can be lost against their will, and which they should therefore not love.

Perhaps one might doubt whether life is somehow taken from the soul when the body is slain. But if it can be taken away, it is of little value; and if it cannot, there is nothing to fear. As for chastity, who would doubt that it is located in the soul itself, since it is a virtue? So it cannot be taken away by a violent assailant. Whatever the one who is killed was going to take away is not completely in our power, so I don't understand how it can be called ours. I don't blame the law that allows such people to be killed; but I can't think of any way to defend those who do the killing.

AUGUSTINE: And I can't think why you are searching for a defense for people whom no law condemns.

EVODIUS: No law, perhaps, of those that are public and are read by human beings; but I suspect that they *are* condemned by a more powerful, hidden law, if indeed there is nothing that is not governed by divine providence. How can they be free of sin in the eyes of that law, when they are defiled with human blood for the sake of things that ought to be held in contempt? It seems to me, therefore, that the law written to govern the people rightly permits these killings and that divine providence avenges them. The law of the people merely institutes penalties sufficient for keeping the peace among ignorant human beings, and only to the extent that their actions can be regulated by human government. But those other faults deserve other penalties that I think Wisdom alone can repeal.

AUGUSTINE: I praise and approve your distinction, for although it is tentative and incomplete, it boldly aims at lofty heights. You think that the law that is established to rule cities allows considerable leeway, leaving many things unpunished that divine providence avenges; and rightly so. And just because that law doesn't do everything, it doesn't follow that we should disapprove of what it does do.

6.   But, if you wish, let us carefully examine to what extent evildoing is punished by the law that rules peoples in this life. Whatever is left is punished inevitably and secretly by divine providence.

EVODIUS: I would like to, if only it were possible to get to the end of such matters; for I think this issue is infinite.

AUGUSTINE: Take heart, and set out confidently and piously in the paths of reason. There is nothing so abstruse or difficult that it cannot become completely clear and straightforward with God's help. And so, depending on him and praying for his aid, let's look into the question that we have posed. First, tell me this: is the law that is promulgated in writing helpful to human beings living this present life?

EVODIUS: Of course, for they are the ones who make up peoples and cities.

AUGUSTINE: Do these human beings and peoples belong to the class of things that are eternal, and can neither change nor perish? Or are they changeable and subject to time?

EVODIUS: Who could doubt that they are changeable and bound by time?

AUGUSTINE: Therefore, if a people is well-ordered and seriousminded, and carefully watches over the common good, and everyone in it values private affairs less than the public interest, is it not right to enact a law that allows this people to choose their own magistrates to look after their interest—that is, the public interest?

EVODIUS: It is quite right.

AUGUSTINE: But suppose that the same people becomes gradually depraved. They come to prefer private interest to the public good. Votes are bought and sold. Corrupted by those who covet honors, they hand over power to wicked and profligate men. In such a case would it not be right for a good and powerful man (if one could be found) to take from this people the power of conferring honors and to limit it to the discretion of a few good people, or even to one?

EVODIUS: Yes, it would.

AUGUSTINE: Now these two laws appear to be contradictory, for one of them gives the people the power to confer honors, while the other takes it away; and the second one is established in such a way that the laws cannot both be in force in one city at the same time. Shall we therefore conclude that one of them is unjust and should not be enacted?

EVODIUS: Not at all.

AUGUSTINE: Then, if you like, let us call a law 'temporal' if, although it is just, it can justly be changed in the course of time.

EVODIUS: Agreed.

AUGUSTINE: Then consider the law that is called the highest reason, which must always be obeyed, and by which the wicked deserve misery and the good deserve a happy life, and by which the law that we agreed to call 'temporal' is rightly enacted and rightly changed. Can anyone of sense deny that this law is unchangeable and eternal? Or can it sometimes be unjust for the wicked to be miserable and the good happy, or for a well-ordered and serious-minded people to choose their own magistrates, while a licentious and worthless people is deprived of this power?

EVODIUS: I see that this law is indeed eternal and unchangeable.

AUGUSTINE: I think you also see that nothing is just and legitimate in the temporal law except that which human beings have derived from the eternal law. For if at one time a people can justly confer honors, and at another time cannot justly do so, this temporal change can be just only because it is derived from the eternal law, according to which it is always just for a serious-minded people to confer honors, but unjust for a frivolous people to do so. Or do you think otherwise?

EVODIUS: I agree.

AUGUSTINE: Then let me briefly explain, to the best of my ability, the notion of the eternal law that is stamped upon our minds: it is the law according to which it is just that all things be perfectly ordered. Tell me if you have some other view.

EVODIUS: I have no objection to make, since what you say is true.

AUGUSTINE: Then since there is this one law, by which all temporal laws regarding human government can be changed, can that law itself be changed in any way?

EVODIUS: I understand that it cannot be changed in any way. For no violent assault, no chance happening, no catastrophe could ever bring it about that it is not just for everything to be perfectly ordered.

7.   AUGUSTINE: Well then, let us now consider what it is for a human being to be perfectly ordered within, since human beings united under one law—a temporal law, as we have said—constitute a people. First, tell me whether you are absolutely certain that you are alive.

EVODIUS: What could I be more certain of than that?

AUGUSTINE: Then can you distinguish between being alive and knowing that you are alive?

EVODIUS: I know that nothing knows it is alive unless it is in fact alive, but I am not sure whether everything that is alive also knows that it is alive.

AUGUSTINE: How I wish you knew, just as you believe, that animals lack reason! Then our discussion would quickly pass over that question. But since you say that you don't know, you are touching off a long discussion. It's not the sort of thing that we can just take for granted and still reach our goal with the logical rigor that I think is needed.

So tell me this. We often see animals that have been tamed by human beings. I don't just mean their bodies; their spirits too are so much under human control that they obey a human will by a kind of instinct and habit. Do you think that there is any way that a wild animal, however strong or ferocious, however keen his senses, could in turn attempt to subdue a human being? Even though it could destroy the human body by open force or by stealth?

EVODIUS: I don't think there is any way that could happen.

AUGUSTINE: Well then, tell me this. It is obvious that many animals easily surpass human beings in strength and in other physical capabilities. So what is it that human beings have in virtue of which they are superior, so that no animal can subdue them, but they can control many animals? Is it not perhaps what is usually called 'reason' or 'understanding'?

EVODIUS: I can't think of anything else, since what makes us superior to animals is in the soul. If they were inanimate, I would say that we are superior to them in virtue of having a soul. But since they are animate, there is something that is present in our souls in virtue of which we are superior, which is lacking in their souls, thus allowing them to be subdued by us. It is obvious to anyone that it is something of considerable importance. What better name for that than 'reason'?

AUGUSTINE: See how easy it is, with God's help, to accomplish something that human beings think is next to impossible. To be honest, I had thought that this question might detain us for as much time as we had spent from the very beginning of this discussion. But in fact, as I understand it, the matter is already settled. So listen now to the next step in the argument. I believe you realize that to know is simply to perceive by means of reason.

EVODIUS: Yes.

AUGUSTINE: So anything that knows it is alive does not lack reason.

EVODIUS: That follows.

AUGUSTINE: But animals are alive, and yet, as has just become clear, they lack reason.

EVODIUS: That is obvious.

AUGUSTINE: So now you know what you previously said you did not know: not everything that is alive knows that it is alive, although everything that knows it is alive must in fact be alive.

EVODIUS: I am quite certain of that now. Pursue the argument further, for you have taught me clearly that it is one thing to be alive and quite another to know that one is alive.

AUGUSTINE: Which of the two do you think is better?

EVODIUS: Clearly, the knowledge that one is alive is better.

AUGUSTINE: You think that the knowledge that one is alive is better than life itself? Perhaps you understand that knowledge is a higher and more genuine sort of life, a life that no one can know unless he understands. And to understand is simply to live a brighter and more perfect life by the light of the mind. So unless I am mistaken, you do not prefer anything else to life; you simply prefer a better life to just any life at all.

EVODIUS: You have understood and explained my view very well indeed. But what if knowledge could sometimes be bad?

AUGUSTINE: I don't think it could, unless we are using 'knowledge' in a broader sense to mean 'experience'. Experience is not always good, since one can experience suffering. But how could knowledge in the strict sense ever be bad, since it is acquired by reason and understanding?

EVODIUS: I accept that distinction. Please continue.

8. AUGUSTINE: Here is what I want to say. Whatever this thing is in virtue of which human beings are superior to animals, whether we should call it 'mind' or 'spirit' or both (for both terms are used in Scripture), if it rules and controls the other things that constitute a human being, then that human being is perfectly ordered. For we see that we have many characteristics in common not only with animals but even with trees and plants. We know that trees, which are at the lowest level of life, take in nourishment, grow, reproduce, and flourish. We recognize and acknowledge that animals can see and hear, and can sense material objects by touch, taste, and smell, often better than we can. Consider also strength, health, and bodily vigor, ease and swiftness of motion. In all of these respects we are superior to some animals, equal to others, and inferior to quite a few. Yet we have these sorts of traits in common with animals, although the life of the lower animals consists entirely in the pursuit of physical pleasures and the avoidance of pains.

There are other qualities that do not appear to exist in animals but are not the highest human attributes: for example, joking and laughing. Anyone with a proper understanding of human nature will consider these things distinctively human, to be sure, but of lesser importance. Then there are traits like the love of praise and fame, and the will to power. Animals do indeed lack these traits, but it should not be thought that an inordinate desire for such things makes us superior to animals. When that drive is not subject to reason it makes us wretched, and no one considers himself superior to another because of his wretchedness.

When these impulses of the soul are ruled by reason, a human being is said to be ordered. For we should not call it right order, or even order at all, when better things are subjected to worse. Don't you agree?

EVODIUS: It is obvious.

AUGUSTINE: Therefore, when reason, mind, or spirit controls the irrational impulses of the soul, a human being is ruled by the very thing that ought to rule according to the law that we have found to be eternal.

EVODIUS: I understand and follow.

AUGUSTINE: Don't you think that a human being disposed and ordered in this way is wise? **9.**

EVODIUS: If this sort of person does not seem wise, I can't think who would.

AUGUSTINE: I believe you also know that many human beings are foolish.

EVODIUS: That's obvious enough.

AUGUSTINE: Now given that fools are the opposite of the wise, and we know what it is to be wise, you should understand perfectly what it is to be a fool.

EVODIUS: Fools, as anyone can tell, are those in whom the mind does not have supreme power.

AUGUSTINE: Then what are we to say about people in this state? Have they no mind? Or is it rather the case that they have a mind, but it doesn't have control of them?

EVODIUS: The latter.

AUGUSTINE: I would very much like to know what evidence you have that a human being has a mind when that mind is not exercising its rightful authority.

EVODIUS: I'd rather have you tackle that question. It's not easy for me to shoulder such a burden.

AUGUSTINE: It is at any rate easy for you to remember what we said a little while ago: animals are tamed and subdued by human beings and serve them. The argument showed that human beings would in turn suffer the same fate at the hands of the animals, were it not for the fact that human beings are superior in a certain respect. Since we found that this was not a *physical* superiority, it was clear that the superiority must be located in the soul. We could find no better name for this than 'reason', which, as we later remembered, is also called 'mind' or 'spirit'. Even if reason and mind are not the same thing, it is surely obvious that only mind can make use of reason. From this we conclude that whatever has reason cannot lack mind.

EVODIUS: I remember that perfectly and acknowledge that it is true.

AUGUSTINE: Do you think that those who tame animals must be wise? For I reserve the term 'wise' for those whom truth demands should be called wise, those who have achieved peace by placing all inordinate desire under the control of the mind.

EVODIUS: It is absurd to think that 'animal trainers', as they are popularly called, or shepherds or cattle-drivers or grooms are wise; yet we see that all of them have control over tame animals and work to gain control of wild animals.

AUGUSTINE: Well there you are; this is solid evidence that a human being can have a mind that lacks control. These people have minds, for they do things that cannot be done without a mind. Yet their minds are not in control, for they are fools. And as we have already established, it is only in the wise that the mind has control.

EVODIUS: It is amazing that we had already agreed on this earlier, and yet I couldn't think how to respond.

10.   But let's continue. Thus far we have found that human wisdom consists in the rule of the human mind, and that it is possible for the mind not to rule.

AUGUSTINE: Do you think that inordinate desire is more powerful than the mind, which we know is granted control over inordinate desires by the eternal law? I do not think so at all, for it would violate perfect order if the weaker controlled the stronger. Therefore, I think the mind must be more powerful than cupidity, precisely because it is right and just for the mind to rule over cupidity.

EVODIUS: I think so too.

AUGUSTINE: And surely we do not doubt that every virtue is superior to every vice, so that the better and more sublime the virtue, the stronger and more invincible it is.

EVODIUS: Who could doubt that?

AUGUSTINE: Then no vicious spirit defeats a spirit armed with virtue.

EVODIUS: Quite correct.

AUGUSTINE: And I don't think you will deny that any sort of spirit is better and more powerful than any material object.

EVODIUS: No one will deny it who sees (as is easy to do) that a living substance is better than a non-living one, and one that gives life is better than one that receives life.

AUGUSTINE: Much less, then, can a material object of any sort overpower a spirit endowed with virtue.

EVODIUS: That is quite obvious.

AUGUSTINE: Can a just spirit, a mind that is preserving its proper right and authority, take another mind that is ruling with the same equity and virtue, drive it from its stronghold, and subject it to inordinate desire?

EVODIUS: Not at all, for two reasons. First, each mind possesses the same degree of excellence. And second, any mind that would attempt such a thing must have already fallen from justice and become vicious, and therefore weaker.

AUGUSTINE: Very sharp. It remains for you to say, if you can, whether you think anything is superior to a rational and wise mind.

EVODIUS: Nothing but God, I think.

AUGUSTINE: That is my view as well. But it is a difficult matter, and this is not the time to attempt to come to understand it, although we hold it most firmly by faith. We must complete our careful and deliberate investigation of the question at hand.

In the present case we can be sure that whatever nature is by **11.** right superior to a mind empowered by virtue, it cannot be an unjust one. Therefore, even if it has the power to do so, it will not force the mind to be a slave to inordinate desire.

EVODIUS: Thus far there is nothing that anyone would have the smallest hesitation about accepting.

AUGUSTINE: The conclusions that we have reached thus far indicate that a mind that is in control, one that possesses virtue, cannot be made a slave to inordinate desire by anything equal or superior to it, because such a thing would be just, or by anything inferior to it, because such a thing would be too weak. Just one possibility remains: only its own will and free choice can make the mind a companion of cupidity.

EVODIUS: I can't see any other alternative.

AUGUSTINE: Then you must also think that the mind justly suffers punishment for so great a sin.

EVODIUS: I cannot deny it.

AUGUSTINE: Surely the very fact that inordinate desire rules the mind is itself no small punishment. Stripped by opposing forces of the splendid wealth of virtue, the mind is dragged by inordinate desire into ruin and poverty; now taking false things for true, and even defending those falsehoods repeatedly; now repudiating what it had once believed and nonetheless rushing headlong into still other falsehoods; now withholding assent and often shying away from clear arguments; now despairing completely of finding the truth and lingering in the shadows of folly; now trying to enter the light of understanding but reeling back in exhaustion.

In the meantime cupidity carries out a reign of terror, buffeting the whole human soul and life with storms coming from every direction. Fear attacks from one side and desire from the other; from one side, anxiety; from the other, an empty and deceptive happiness; from one side, the agony of losing what one loved; from the other, the passion to acquire what one did not have; from one side, the pain of an injury received; from the other, the burning desire to avenge it. Wherever you turn, avarice can pinch, extravagance squander, ambition destroy, pride swell, envy torment, apathy crush, obstinacy incite, oppression chafe, and countless other evils crowd the realm of inordinate desire and run riot. In short, can we consider this punishment trivial—a punishment that, as you realize, all who do not cleave to wisdom must suffer?

EVODIUS: It is indeed a great punishment, I think, and a perfectly just one, if someone chooses to descend from the heights of wisdom and become a slave to inordinate desire. But it's not clear whether there can be anyone who wills or ever did will to do so. We do, of course, *believe* that human beings were created perfectly by God and established in a happy life, so that it is by their own will that they have fallen from happiness into the hardships of mortal life. Nonetheless, although I believe this most firmly, I have not yet understood it. So if you decide that we should postpone a careful investigation of this issue, I would be most reluctant to do so.

12.   The question that troubles me most is this: We are certainly fools and have never been wise. And yet we are said to suffer such bitter penalties deservedly because we abandoned the stronghold of virtue and chose to be slaves to inordinate desire. How can this be? I simply will not allow you to postpone solving this problem, if you can.

AUGUSTINE: You speak as if you knew for certain that we have never been wise, for you are thinking only of the time since we were born into this life. But since wisdom is in the soul, it is important to ask whether the soul enjoyed another sort of life before its association with the body. Perhaps it lived wisely at that time. This is a big question and a great mystery, one that we should discuss in its proper place.[7] Nonetheless, that difficulty

---

7. Augustine takes up a closely related question in Book Three, chapters 20 and 21.

will not prevent us from answering the question at hand as well as we can. So tell me this: Do we have a will?

EVODIUS: I don't know.

AUGUSTINE: Do you want to know?

EVODIUS: I don't know that either.

AUGUSTINE: Then don't ask me any more questions.

EVODIUS: Why not?

AUGUSTINE: First, because there's no reason for me to answer your questions unless you want to know the answer. Second, because I should not discuss these sorts of things with you unless you want to attain wisdom. And finally, because you can't be my friend unless you want things to go well for me. But surely you have already seen whether you will your own happiness.

EVODIUS: You're right; it can't be denied that we have a will. Do go on—let's see what you deduce from that fact.

AUGUSTINE: I shall. But first tell me whether you think you have a good will.

EVODIUS: What is a good will?

AUGUSTINE: It is a will by which we desire to live upright and honorable lives and to attain the highest wisdom. So just ask yourself: Do you desire an upright and honorable life and fervently will to be wise? And is it indisputable that when we will these things, we have a good will?

EVODIUS: My answer to both questions is yes. I now admit that I have not just a will, but a good will.

AUGUSTINE: How highly do you value this will? You surely do not think it should be compared with wealth or honors or physical pleasures, or even all of these together.

EVODIUS: God forbid such wicked madness!

AUGUSTINE: Then should we not rejoice a little that we have something in our souls—this very thing that I call a good will—in comparison with which those things we mentioned are utterly worthless, things that a great many human beings will spare no effort and shirk no danger to obtain?

EVODIUS: Indeed, we should rejoice greatly.

AUGUSTINE: Then do you think that those who do not attain such joy suffer a small loss by missing so great a good?

EVODIUS: It is a great loss.

AUGUSTINE: Then I believe you realize that it is up to our will whether we enjoy or lack such a great and true good. For what is so much in the power of the will as the will itself? To have a good will is to have something far more valuable than all earthly kingdoms and pleasures; to lack it is to lack something that only the will itself can give, something that is better than all the goods that are not in our power. Some people consider themselves utterly miserable if they do not achieve a splendid reputation, great wealth, and various goods of the body. But don't you consider them utterly miserable, even if they have all these things, when they cleave to things that they can quite easily lose, things that they do not have simply in virtue of willing them, while they lack a good will, which is incomparably better than those things and yet, even though it is such a great good, can be theirs if only they will to have it?

Evodius: I certainly do.

Augustine: Then fools, even if they were never wise (which is a doubtful and obscure issue), are justly and deservedly afflicted with such misery.

Evodius: I agree.

13. Augustine: Now do you think that prudence is the knowledge of what is to be desired and what is to be avoided?

Evodius: Yes.

Augustine: And isn't fortitude the disposition of the soul by which we have no fear of misfortune or of the loss of things that are not in our power?

Evodius: It is.

Augustine: And temperance is the disposition that checks and restrains the desire for things that it is wicked to desire. Don't you agree?

Evodius: Yes, I do.

Augustine: And justice, finally, is the virtue by which all people are given their due.

Evodius: That is exactly my conception of justice.

Augustine: Then consider those who have this good will whose excellence we have been discussing for so long now. They lovingly embrace this one unsurpassable good and delight in its presence. They enjoy it to the full and rejoice when they consider that so great a good is theirs and cannot be stolen or taken away from them against their will. Can we doubt that they will resist everything that is inimical to this one good?

Evodius: Indeed they must resist such things.

AUGUSTINE: Then they are surely endowed with prudence, since they realize that the good is to be desired and everything inimical to it is to be avoided.

EVODIUS: I don't think anyone could realize that unless he had prudence.

AUGUSTINE: Exactly. And how can we not attribute fortitude to them as well? For they neither love nor value things that are not in our power. Such things are loved by an evil will, which they must resist as an enemy of their own most beloved good. And since they do not love such things, they consider them utterly worthless and are not pained by losing them. And this, as we said earlier, is the role of fortitude.

EVODIUS: Then we must attribute fortitude to them. For I can't imagine anyone who deserves to be called strong[8] if not those who patiently and calmly bear the absence of those things that it is not in our power to obtain or to keep, as we have found that those who have a good will must necessarily do.

AUGUSTINE: Now consider whether we can deny them temperance, which is the virtue that restrains inordinate desires. For what is more harmful to a good will than inordinate desire? So you may conclude that those who love their own good will resist and oppose inordinate desires in every way they can, and so they are rightly called temperate.

EVODIUS: I agree. Please continue.

AUGUSTINE: Finally comes justice. I don't see how they could lack justice, since those who have and cherish a good will, and resist whatever is inimical to that will, as we have said, cannot wish anyone ill. Therefore they harm no one, which in turn implies that they give all people their due. And I believe you remember agreeing when I said that this is the role of justice.

EVODIUS: I do remember, and I acknowledge that all four virtues that you just described, with my agreement, are present in those who love their own good will and value it highly.

AUGUSTINE: What is to keep us from saying that the lives of such people are praiseworthy?

EVODIUS: Nothing at all. Indeed, all of these considerations urge us, even compel us, to say so.

---

8. In Latin, *fortis*, the root of *fortitudo* ("fortitude")

AUGUSTINE: Now can you deny that one ought to avoid an unhappy life?

EVODIUS: I am firmly convinced that that is exactly what one ought to do.

AUGUSTINE: And of course you don't think that what is praiseworthy should be avoided.

EVODIUS: I think it should be diligently sought after.

AUGUSTINE: Then a praiseworthy life is not unhappy.

EVODIUS: That follows.

AUGUSTINE: Then I believe you can easily admit that this life, which is not unhappy, is in fact the happy life.

EVODIUS: That is quite obvious.

AUGUSTINE: Then it is established that people are happy when they love their own good will, in comparison with which they scorn everything that is called good but can be lost even though one wills to retain it.

EVODIUS: Of course. That follows from the points we made earlier.

AUGUSTINE: Quite correct. But tell me this: When they love their own good will and value it as highly as we have said, doesn't that in itself constitute a good will?

EVODIUS: Yes, it does.

AUGUSTINE: And if we are right in thinking that such people are happy, doesn't it follow that those who have the opposite sort of will are unhappy?

EVODIUS: Certainly.

AUGUSTINE: Then why should we hesitate to affirm that, even if we have never been wise, it is by the will that we lead and deserve a praiseworthy and happy life, or a contemptible and unhappy one?

EVODIUS: Indeed, the conclusions we have reached are quite certain and indubitable.

AUGUSTINE: Consider another point. I believe you recall the way in which we defined a good will: it is a will by which we desire to live upright and honorable lives.

EVODIUS: I remember that.

AUGUSTINE: So if by our good will we love and embrace that will, and prefer it to everything that we cannot retain simply by willing to retain it, then, as the argument showed, we will possess those very virtues that constitute an upright and honorable life. From this it follows that all who will to live upright and honorable lives, if they will this more than they will transitory goods, attain such a great good so easily that they have it by the very act of willing to have it.

EVODIUS: I can hardly keep myself from shouting for joy that such a great and easily attainable good has suddenly sprung up within me.

AUGUSTINE: And when that very joy, born of the attainment of this good, calmly, quietly, and steadily bears up the soul, this is called the happy life. For doesn't a happy life consist precisely in the enjoyment of true and unshakable goods?

EVODIUS: Indeed it does.

AUGUSTINE: Good. But do you think that there is anyone who **14.** does not in every way will and desire a happy life?

EVODIUS: Clearly, every human being wills that.

AUGUSTINE: Then why doesn't everyone attain it? We have found that it is by the will that human beings deserve, and therefore receive, either a happy or an unhappy life. There's a sort of contradiction here; unless we take great care to examine it, it will undermine our careful and persuasive argument. How can anyone suffer an unhappy life by the will, when absolutely no one wills to be unhappy? Or to put it another way, how can we claim that it is by the will that human beings achieve a happy life, when so many are unhappy despite the fact that everyone wills to be happy?

Perhaps it is because it is one thing to will rightly or wrongly, and quite another to deserve something because of a good or bad will. Those who are happy, who must also be good, are not happy simply because they will to be happy—even the wicked will that—but because they will it in the right way, whereas the wicked do not. So it's no surprise that unhappy human beings do not attain the happy life that they will. For they do not likewise will the one thing that goes along with the happy life, without which no one attains it or is worthy to attain it—and that is, to live rightly. For the eternal law (to which it is time for us to return) has established with unshakable firmness that the will is rewarded with happiness or punished with unhappiness depending on its merit. And so when we say that it is by the will that human beings are unhappy, we don't mean that they will to be unhappy, but that their will is in such a state that unhappiness must follow whether they will it or not. So it does not contradict our earlier argument to say that everyone wills to be happy but not everyone can be; for not everyone has the will to live rightly, which must accompany the will to live happily. Or do you have some objection to make?

EVODIUS: None at all.

15.   But let's see how this relates to the question about the two laws.[9]

AUGUSTINE: Very well. First, tell me something about those who delight in living rightly, and take such pleasure in it that they find it not merely right but actually sweet and joyful. Do they love and cherish the law that, as they see, confers a happy life upon a good will and an unhappy life upon an evil will?

EVODIUS: They love it intensely, for it is by following that law that they live as they do.

AUGUSTINE: Now when they love this, are they loving something changeable and temporal, or something stable and eternal?

EVODIUS: Clearly, something eternal and unchangeable.

AUGUSTINE: What about those who persevere in an evil will but nonetheless desire to be happy? Can they love the law by which such people are justly punished with unhappiness?

EVODIUS: Not at all, I think.

AUGUSTINE: Do they love something else?

EVODIUS: A number of things—whatever their evil will is bent on getting or keeping.

AUGUSTINE: I believe you mean things like wealth, honors, pleasures, physical beauty, and everything else that one cannot get or keep simply by willing.

EVODIUS: That is exactly what I meant.

AUGUSTINE: You surely do not think that these things are eternal, subject as they are to the ravages of time.

EVODIUS: Only a complete fool could think that.

AUGUSTINE: Then it is clear that some human beings love eternal things while others love temporal things; and we have also found that there are two laws, one eternal and one temporal. Now if you know anything about justice, which human beings do you think should be subject to the eternal law, and which should be subject to the temporal?

9. That is, the question posed at the beginning of chapter 6: To what extent does the temporal law punish evildoing?

EVODIUS: The answer to that is obvious. I think that those who are happy on account of their love for eternal things live under the eternal law, while those who are unhappy are subject to the temporal law.

AUGUSTINE: You're correct, provided that you remain firm in holding what our argument clearly demonstrated: that those who serve the temporal law cannot be free from the eternal law, from which is derived, as we said, everything that is just and yet can justly be changed. But I believe you realize that those who cleave to the eternal law by their good will have no need of the temporal law.

EVODIUS: I agree.

AUGUSTINE: So the eternal law demands that we purify our love by turning it away from temporal things and toward what is eternal.

EVODIUS: Yes.

AUGUSTINE: But when human beings in their cupidity cleave to things that can be called ours only for a time, the temporal law demands that they possess those things in accordance with the law by which peace and human society are preserved—insofar as they *can* be preserved on the basis of such things. The first such good is this body, along with all of the things associated with it that are called goods, such as health, keen senses, strength, beauty, and other qualities, some of which are necessary for good deeds and are therefore to be regarded highly, and others of which are less valuable. The second such good is freedom. Now the only genuine freedom is that possessed by those who are happy and cleave to the eternal law; but I am talking about the sort of freedom that people have in mind when they think they are free because they have no human masters, or that people desire when they want to be set free by their masters. Then come parents, brothers and sisters, a spouse, children, neighbors, relatives, friends, and anyone who is bound to us by some need. Next is the city itself, which frequently takes the place of the parents, together with honors and praise and what is called popular acclaim. And finally comes property, which includes anything over which the law gives us control and which we have a recognized right to sell or give away.

To explain how the law distributes all of these things to their rightful owners is a long and difficult task, and one that is clearly irrelevant to the matter at hand. It is enough to see that the temporal law can punish evildoing only by taking away one or another of these goods from the one being punished. So it is by fear that the temporal law coerces human beings and bends the souls of its subjects in whatever direction it pleases. As long as they are afraid of losing these things, they use them with the kind of moderation necessary to maintain whatever sort of city can be built out of such people. They are punished, not because they love temporal goods, but because they wrongfully take them away from others. Now see if we haven't reached the end of the question that you thought was infinite. For we set out to discover the extent to which the law that governs earthly peoples and cities has the power to avenge evildoing.

EVODIUS: I see that we have indeed reached the end.

AUGUSTINE: Then you also see this: whether this punishment is inflicted by an unjust act or by just retribution, it would be no punishment at all if human beings did not love things that can be lost against their will.

EVODIUS: I see that as well.

AUGUSTINE: Therefore, the very same things are used in different ways by different people; some use them badly and others use them well. Someone who uses them badly clings to them and becomes entangled with them. He serves things that ought to serve him, fixing on goods that he cannot even use properly because he is not himself good. But one who uses these things rightly shows that they are good, although not good for himself. For those things do not make the one who uses them good or better; in fact, they become good by being put to good use. And so someone who uses them well does not become attached to them. They don't become limbs of his soul, as it were (which is what happens when one loves them), so that when these things begin to be amputated he is not disfigured by any pain or decay. He is completely above such things, ready to possess and make use of them when there is need, and even readier to lose them and do without them. Since this is the case, you must realize that we should not find fault with silver and gold because of the greedy, or food because of gluttons, or wine because of drunkards, or womanly beauty because of fornicators and adulterers, and so on, especially since you know that fire can be used to heal and bread to poison.

EVODIUS: Clearly we must not blame the things themselves but the people that use them wrongly.

AUGUSTINE: That's right. We have now, I think, begun to see what **16.** the eternal law can do. We have found out how far the temporal law can go in punishing evildoing. We have clearly and carefully distinguished between two sorts of things—eternal and temporal; and in turn between two sorts of human beings—those who pursue and love eternal things, and those who pursue and love temporal things. We have determined that the choice to follow and embrace one or the other lies with the will, and that only the will can depose the mind from its stronghold of power and deprive it of right order. And it has become clear that we should not blame anything when someone uses it wrongly; we should blame the one who uses it wrongly. Given all of that, why don't we return to the question we posed at the beginning of this discussion and see whether it has been answered.

We set out to discover what evildoing is. This whole discussion was aimed at answering that question. So we are now in a position to ask whether evildoing is anything other than neglecting eternal things, which the mind perceives and enjoys by means of itself and which it cannot lose if it loves them; and instead pursuing temporal things—which are perceived by means of the body, the least valuable part of a human being, and which can never be certain—as if they were great and marvelous things. It seems to me that all evil deeds—that is, all sins—fall into this one category. But I want to know what you think about this.

EVODIUS: I agree; all sins come about when someone turns away from divine things that truly persist and toward changeable and uncertain things. These things do have their proper place, and they have a certain beauty of their own; but when a perverse and disordered soul pursues them it becomes enslaved to the very things that divine order and law command it to rule over.

And I think that we have answered another question. After we asked what evildoing is, we set out to discover the source of our evildoing. Now unless I am mistaken, our argument showed that we do evil by the free choice of the will. But I have a further question. Since, as we have found, free choice gives us the ability to sin, should it have been given to us by the one who created us? It would seem that we would not have sinned if we had lacked free choice, so there is still the danger that God might turn out to be the cause of our evil deeds.

AUGUSTINE: Don't let that bother you. We will take that up sometime when we can deal with it more carefully. It is time to bring this discussion to a close. I want you to believe that we have been knocking on the doors of great and hidden questions. When we begin to enter their inner chambers, with God as our guide, you will see what a great difference there is between this discussion and those that will follow, and how superior they are not only in the shrewdness of the investigation but also in the majesty of the subject matter and the clearest light of truth. May piety assist us, so that divine providence will allow us to keep on course and complete our investigation.

EVODIUS: I yield to your will, and I gladly join you in your decision and in your prayer.

Book Two

EVODIUS: Now explain to me, if you can, why God gave human **1.** beings free choice of the will, since if we had not received it, we would not have been able to sin.

AUGUSTINE: Do you know for certain that God gave us this thing that you think should not have been given?

EVODIUS: If I understood Book One correctly, we have free choice of the will and we cannot sin without it.

AUGUSTINE: I too remember that that had become quite clear to us. But what I asked just now was whether you knew that it was *God* who gave us this thing, which we clearly have and by which we sin.

EVODIUS: Who else would it be? For we have our existence from God, and it is from him that we deserve punishment for doing wrong and reward for doing good.

AUGUSTINE: Here again I want to know whether you know this for certain, or whether you willingly believe it on the urging of some authority, without actually knowing it.

EVODIUS: I admit that at first I believed this on authority. But what could be truer than that everything good comes from God, that everything just is good, and that it is just for sinners to be punished and the good rewarded? From this I conclude that it is God who afflicts sinners with unhappiness and confers happiness on the good.

AUGUSTINE: I make no objection. But I do have one further question: How do you know that we have our existence from God? You did not explain that; you showed only that it is from him that we deserve punishment or reward.

EVODIUS: That is an obvious consequence of the fact that God, as the source of all justice, punishes sins. It may be that goodness confers benefits on those not committed to its charge, but justice does not punish those not in its jurisdiction. So it is obvious that we belong to God, because he is not only most generous in conferring benefits but also most just in punishing.

Furthermore, I claimed, and you agreed, that everything good is from God. From this we can understand that human beings too are from God. For human beings as such are good things, since they can live rightly if they so will.

29

AUGUSTINE: If all of this is true, the question you posed has clearly been answered. If human beings are good things, and they cannot do right unless they so will, then they ought to have a free will, without which they cannot do right. True, they can also use free will to sin, but we should not therefore believe that God gave them free will so that they would be able to sin. The fact that human beings could not live rightly without it was sufficient reason for God to give it. The very fact that anyone who uses free will to sin is divinely punished shows that free will was given to enable human beings to live rightly, for such punishment would be unjust if free will had been given both for living rightly and for sinning. After all, how could someone justly be punished for using the will for the very purpose for which it was given? When God punishes a sinner, don't you think he is saying, "Why didn't you use your free will for the purpose for which I gave it to you?"—that is, for living rightly?

And as for the goodness that we so admired in God's justice—his punishing sins and rewarding good deeds—how could it even exist if human beings lacked the free choice of the will? No action would be either a sin or a good deed if it were not performed by the will, and so both punishment and reward would be unjust if human beings had no free will. But it was right for there to be justice in both reward and punishment, since this is one of the goods that come from God. Therefore, it was right for God to give free will to human beings.

2. EVODIUS: I concede that point now. But don't you think that if free will was given to us for living rightly, we ought not to have been able to pervert it and use it for sinning? It should have been like justice, which was also given to human beings to enable them to live well. No one can use justice to live wickedly. In the same way, it ought to be the case that no one could use the will to sin, if indeed the will was given for acting rightly.

AUGUSTINE: God will, I hope, enable me to reply to you—or rather, he will enable you to reply to yourself, as Truth, the greatest teacher of all, teaches you within. But first I want you to tell me this. I asked whether you knew for certain that God gave us free will, and you said that you did. So now that we have agreed that he gave us free will, should we presume to say that it should not have been given? If there is some doubt whether it was God who gave it, it is appropriate for us to ask whether it

was a good gift; and if we find that it was, then we have also
found that it was given by God, from whom the soul has all good
gifts. But if we find that it was not a good gift, we will understand
that it was not given by God, whom it is impious to blame. But
if it is quite certain that God gave us free will, then we must
admit that it ought to have been given, and in exactly the way
that it was given; for God gave it, and his deeds are utterly beyond
reproach.

EVODIUS: Although I hold these things with unshaken faith, let's
investigate them as if they were all uncertain, since I do not yet
know them. It is uncertain whether free will was given for doing
right, since we can also use it to sin; consequently, it is also
uncertain whether it ought to have been given. For if it is uncertain
whether it was given for doing right, then it is also uncertain
whether it ought to have been given. This means in turn that it
is doubtful whether it was given by God. For if it is doubtful
whether it ought to have been given, then it is also doubtful
whether it was given by God, since it is impious to believe that
God gave something that should not have been given.

AUGUSTINE: You are at any rate certain that God exists.

EVODIUS: Even that is something I hold by faith, not something
I see for myself.

AUGUSTINE: Scripture says, "The fool has said in his heart, 'There
is no God'."[1] Suppose one of those fools were to say that to you.
Suppose he did not want to believe what you believe, but to know
whether what you believe is true. Would you just give up, or
would you think that he could somehow be persuaded of what
you firmly believe—especially if he was not merely being contentious, but sincerely wanted to know?

EVODIUS: This last proviso of yours suggests a response. However
absurd he might be, he would surely concede that one should
not discuss anything, and especially not such an important matter,
with a deceitful and obstinate person. Then he would have to get
me to believe that he had the proper attitude and was not conceal-
ing any deceitfulness or obstinacy regarding this issue. Then I
would point out to him that he expects other people to believe
things about his own state of mind, things that he knows but

1. Psalm 14:1; 53:1

other people do not. And I would try to get him to see (as I think anyone easily can) how much more reasonable it is for him to believe that God exists on the authority of the writings of such great men, who left written testimony that they lived with the Son of God, and wrote that they saw things that could not have happened if God did not exist. He would be completely foolish to reproach me for believing them, when he expects me to believe him. And since he could not rightly reproach me, he would have no reason not to join me.

AUGUSTINE: But if you think it is acceptable to believe that God exists because we have found those men to be reliable authorities, why don't you think we should also accept the authority of those same men regarding the other issues that we had found to be uncertain and unknown, rather than toiling on with our inquiry?

EVODIUS: But we want to know and understand what we believe.

AUGUSTINE: Your memory serves you well; we cannot deny what we said at the beginning of our previous discussion. Unless believing and understanding were two different things, and we were first to believe the great and divine things that we desire to understand, there would have been no point in the prophet's saying "Unless you believe, you will not understand."[2] At first our Lord himself by his words and deeds urged those whom he had called to salvation to believe in him. But later, when he spoke of the gift that he was going to give to those who believed, he did not say, "This is eternal life, that they may *believe*," but "This is eternal life, that they may *know* you, the true God, and him whom you have sent, Jesus Christ."[3] And he said to those who already believe, "Seek, and you will find."[4] For something that is believed but not known has not yet been found, and no one becomes ready to find God unless he first believes what he will afterwards know.

Therefore, let us diligently obey the Lord's command as we seek; for he himself will show us what we seek at his urging, insofar as it can be found in this life by such people as we are. For we must believe that better people, even in this earthly life, and all good and pious people in the next, see and possess these

2. Isaiah 7:9 (pre-Vulgate text)
3. John 17:3
4. Matthew 7:7

things more clearly and completely. We must hope one day to be like them, and we must wholeheartedly desire and love these things and place no value on what is earthly and human.

But if you don't mind, let's pose our questions in the following **3.** order. First, how is it manifest that God exists? Second, do all things, insofar as they are good, come from God? And finally, should free will be counted as one of those good things? Once we have answered those questions it will, I think, be clear whether free will ought to have been given to human beings. So to take something quite obvious as our starting point, I will first ask you whether you yourself exist. Or do you perhaps fear that you might be mistaken even about that? Yet you could certainly not be mistaken unless you existed.

EVODIUS: Yes; do go on.

AUGUSTINE: Well then, since it is obvious that you exist, and this could not be obvious unless you were alive, it is also obvious that you are alive. Do you understand that these two things are absolutely true?

EVODIUS: I understand completely.

AUGUSTINE: Then a third thing is obvious, namely, that you understand.

EVODIUS: Yes.

AUGUSTINE: Which of these three do you think is superior?

EVODIUS: Understanding.

AUGUSTINE: Why do you think so?

EVODIUS: Because there are these three things: existence, life, and understanding. A stone exists, and an animal is alive, but I do not think that a stone is alive or an animal understands. But whatever understands must certainly also exist and be alive. So I do not hesitate to conclude that something in which all three are present is superior to something that lacks any of them. For whatever is alive also exists, but it does not follow that it also understands; such, I think, is the life of an animal. But from the fact that something exists it does not follow that it is alive and understands; for I can admit that corpses exist, but no one would say that they are alive. And whatever is not alive can certainly not understand.

AUGUSTINE: So we hold that corpses lack two of these characteristics, animals lack one, and human beings lack none.

EVODIUS: Yes.

AUGUSTINE: And we hold that the most valuable of these three is the one that human beings have in addition to the other two, that is, understanding; for whatever understands must also exist and be alive.

EVODIUS: Yes.

AUGUSTINE: Now tell me whether you know that you have the familiar bodily senses: sight, hearing, smell, taste, and touch.

EVODIUS: I do.

AUGUSTINE: What do you think pertains to the sense of sight? That is, what do you think we perceive by means of sight?

EVODIUS: All material objects.

AUGUSTINE: But we don't sense hard and soft by sight, do we?

EVODIUS: No.

AUGUSTINE: So what object of perception pertains specifically to the eyes?

EVODIUS: Color.

AUGUSTINE: And to the ears?

EVODIUS: Sound.

AUGUSTINE: And to smell?

EVODIUS: Odor.

AUGUSTINE: And to taste?

EVODIUS: Flavor.

AUGUSTINE: And to touch?

EVODIUS: Hard and soft, rough and smooth, and many such things.

AUGUSTINE: But what about the shapes of material objects—large, small, square, round, and so on? Can't we perceive them both by touch and by sight? So they cannot be attributed exclusively to sight or to touch; they pertain to both.

EVODIUS: I understand that.

AUGUSTINE: Then you also understand that some objects are perceived exclusively by one sense, while others can be perceived by more than one.

EVODIUS: Yes.

AUGUSTINE: But can we by any of our senses determine what belongs to just one sense and what to more than one?

EVODIUS: Not at all; we determine that by a kind of inner sense.

AUGUSTINE: But surely that inner sense is not reason itself, which animals do not have. For it is, I think, by reason that we understand these things and recognize that they are so.

EVODIUS: Actually, I think that by reason we understand that we have a kind of inner sense to which everything is conveyed from those five familiar senses. An animal's sense of sight is one thing; the sense by which it either avoids or pursues what it sees is quite another. Sight is in the eyes; the other sense is in the soul. By it animals either pursue and accept what gives them pleasure or avoid and reject what gives them pain, whether these things are the objects of sight or of hearing or of the other bodily senses. This inner sense is itself neither sight nor hearing nor smell nor taste nor touch; it is some other thing that presides over all of them. Although we understand this sense by means of reason, as I said, we cannot identify it with reason itself, since it is clearly present in beasts.

AUGUSTINE: I agree that there is such a thing, and I do not hesitate to call it "the inner sense." But unless the things that the bodily senses convey to us get beyond the inner sense, we can never attain knowledge. For we know only what we grasp by reason. And we know, for example, that colors cannot be perceived by hearing nor sounds by sight. We do not know this by means of the eyes or ears, or by that inner sense, which even animals have. For we must not think that animals know that the ears cannot perceive light nor the eyes sound, since we come to know that only by rational attention and thought.

EVODIUS: I can't say that I quite see that. What if animals do in fact use that inner sense, which you admit they have, to judge that colors cannot be perceived by hearing nor sound by sight?

AUGUSTINE: Surely you do not think that they can distinguish between the color that is perceived, the sense that exists in the eyes, the inner sense within the soul, and reason, by which each of these is defined and enumerated.

EVODIUS: Not at all.

AUGUSTINE: Could reason thus distinguish between these four things and provide them with definitions unless each of them were in some way conveyed to reason? Color is conveyed to reason through the sense of the eyes; that sense in turn is conveyed through the inner sense that presides over it; and the inner sense is conveyed through itself, at least if nothing interferes.

EVODIUS: I don't see how else it could be.

AUGUSTINE: Do you see that we perceive color by means of the sense of the eyes, but we do not perceive that sense by means of itself? For the sense that you use to see color is not the same sense that you use to see seeing itself.

EVODIUS: Not at all.

AUGUSTINE: Try to make a further distinction. I believe you will not deny that color is one thing and seeing color another; and it is yet another thing to have a sense by which one could see colors if they were present, even though no colors do happen to be present at the moment.

EVODIUS: I distinguish between these things and admit that each is different from the other two.

AUGUSTINE: Which of these three do you see with your eyes? Is it not color?

EVODIUS: It is.

AUGUSTINE: Then tell me how you see the other two—for you could not distinguish between them unless you saw them.

EVODIUS: I don't know how. I know that some such power exists, nothing more.

AUGUSTINE: Then you don't know whether it is reason itself; or that life that we call the "inner sense," which surpasses the senses of the body; or some other thing?

EVODIUS: No.

AUGUSTINE: But you do know that reason alone can define these things, and that reason can do this only for things that are presented to it for consideration.

EVODIUS: Certainly.

AUGUSTINE: So whatever this thing is by which we perceive everything we know, it is an agent of reason. It takes whatever it comes into contact with and presents that to reason so that reason can delimit the things that are perceived and grasp them by knowledge and not merely by sense.

EVODIUS: Yes.

AUGUSTINE: Then what about reason itself, which distinguishes between its agents and the things that they convey, which understands the difference between itself and them, and which affirms that it is itself far more powerful than they are? Surely reason does not grasp itself by anything other than itself, that is, by anything other than reason. How else would you know that you had reason, unless you perceived it by reason?

EVODIUS: Quite right.

AUGUSTINE: Now when we perceive color, we do not by that

same sense perceive that we are perceiving. When we hear a sound, we do not hear our sense of hearing. When we smell a rose, we do not also smell our sense of smell. When we taste something, we do not also taste the sense of taste. When we touch something, we cannot also touch the sense of touch. It is therefore obvious that none of the five senses can perceive itself, although all of them can perceive material objects.

EVODIUS: That is obvious.

AUGUSTINE: I think it is also obvious that not only does the inner **4.** sense perceive what it receives from the five bodily senses, but it also perceives the senses themselves. An animal would not move to pursue or flee from something unless it perceived the fact that it was perceiving, and it cannot perceive that fact by any of the five senses. This perception does not amount to knowledge, since only reason can produce knowledge; but it does suffice to move the animal. Now if this is still unclear, it will help if you consider one specific sense. Take sight as an example. The animal could never open its eyes and look around to find what it wanted to see unless it perceived that it did not see that thing with its eyes closed or stationary. But if it perceives that it does not see when it is not seeing, it must also perceive that it does see when it is seeing, because the same appetite that makes it look around when it does not see makes it keep looking the same way when it does see. This shows that it perceives both.

But it is not so clear whether this life, which perceives that it perceives material objects, also perceives itself—except that everyone who considers the matter will realize that every living thing flees from death. Since death is the opposite of life, it must be the case that life perceives itself, because it flees from its opposite. But if this is not yet clear, disregard it, so that we can proceed to our goal solely on the basis of certain and obvious truths. The following truths are obvious: The bodily senses perceive material objects. No bodily sense can perceive itself. The inner sense, however, perceives material objects through the bodily senses and also perceives the bodily senses themselves. And by reason all of these things, as well as reason itself, become known and are part of knowledge. Don't you think so?

EVODIUS: Yes.

AUGUSTINE: Now then, what about this question we have already spent so much time trying to answer?

5. EVODIUS: As far as I remember, we are now dealing with the first of the three questions that we posed a little while ago to give coherence and order to this discussion; that is, although we must firmly and steadfastly believe that God exists, how can this fact be made manifest?

AUGUSTINE: Your memory serves you well. But I also want you to remember that when I asked you whether you knew that you yourself exist, we found that you knew not only this fact but two others.

EVODIUS: I remember that too.

AUGUSTINE: Which of the three includes everything that the bodily senses perceive? That is, in which category do you think we should place everything that we perceive by means of the eyes or any other bodily organ: in that which merely exists, in that which is also alive, or in that which also understands?

EVODIUS: In that which merely exists.

AUGUSTINE: What about sense itself? To which category does it belong?

EVODIUS: To that which is alive.

AUGUSTINE: Which of these two do you think is better: sense, or the thing that sense perceives?

EVODIUS: Sense, of course.

AUGUSTINE: Why?

EVODIUS: Because something that is alive is better than something that merely exists.

AUGUSTINE: Then what about the inner sense, which, as we found earlier, is lower than reason and is present both in us and in animals? Do you doubt that it is superior to the sense by which we perceive material objects, which is in turn superior to those material objects?

EVODIUS: Not at all.

AUGUSTINE: I want you to tell me why not. You can't very well say that the inner sense belongs to the category of things that understand; it belongs to the category of things that exist and are alive but lack understanding. For the inner sense is present even in animals, which lack understanding. Given that, I ask why you consider the inner sense superior to the sense by which we perceive material objects, since both belong to the category of things that are alive. You said that the sense that perceives material objects is superior to the objects that it perceives, because material objects belong to the category of things that merely exist, whereas sense belongs to the category of things that are also alive; but since the inner sense also belongs to this category, tell me why you think it is better. Perhaps you will say that this is because the inner sense perceives the bodily senses, but I don't think you are going to find any trustworthy rule stating that whatever perceives is better than the thing perceived. Such a rule might force us to say that whatever understands is better than the thing understood, which is false; human beings understand wisdom, but they are not better than wisdom. Therefore, see if you can explain why you thought that the inner sense is superior to the sense by which we perceive material objects.

Evodius: I think so because I know that the inner sense is a kind of controller or judge of the bodily sense. If the bodily sense falls short in performing its duty, the inner sense demands that its agent make good on this debt, as we discussed a little while ago. The sense of the eye does not see whether it is seeing or not, and so it cannot judge what it lacks or what is enough. That is the job of the inner sense, which warns even the soul of an animal to open its eyes and make up for what it perceives is missing. And everyone realizes that the judge is superior to the thing judged.

Augustine: Do you also realize that the bodily sense also judges material objects in a certain way? For it feels pleasure or pain, depending on whether it is affected gently or harshly by the material object. Just as the inner sense judges what is adequate or inadequate in the sense of the eyes, so the sense of the eyes judges what is adequate or inadequate in colors. In the same way, just as the inner sense judges whether our hearing is sufficiently attentive or not, hearing itself judges whether sounds are pleasant or unpleasant. There's no need to go on to the other senses. I believe you already understand what I am trying to say: just as the inner sense judges the bodily senses when it approves their completeness or demands what is lacking, so the bodily senses judge material objects by accepting what is pleasing and rejecting what is not.

Evodius: I understand, and I concede that all of this is quite true.

Augustine: Our next subject is whether reason judges the inner sense. I won't ask whether reason is *better* than the inner sense, since I have no doubt that you think it is. And actually, I don't think we even need to ask whether reason judges the inner sense. Just consider all we know about the things that are below reason: material objects, the bodily senses, and the inner sense. How could we know that one is better than another, and that reason is more excellent than any of them, unless reason itself told us? And reason could not tell us this unless it judged all of these things.

EVODIUS: Clearly.

AUGUSTINE: So a nature that has existence but not life or understanding, like an inanimate body, is inferior to a nature that has both existence and life but not understanding, like the souls of animals; and such a thing is in turn inferior to something that has all three, like the rational mind of a human being. Given that, do you think that you could find anything in us—that is, anything that is part of our human nature—more excellent than understanding? It is clear that we have a body, as well as a sort of life by which the body is animated and nourished; both of these we find in animals. We also have a third thing, like the head or eye of the soul, or however reason and understanding might be more aptly described; and this, animals do not have. So I ask you: can you think of anything in human nature more exalted than reason?

EVODIUS: Nothing at all.

AUGUSTINE: What if we could find something that you were certain not only exists, but is more excellent than our reason? Would you hesitate to say that this thing, whatever it is, is God?

EVODIUS: Even if I found something better than the best part of my nature, I would not immediately say that it was God. What I call 'God' is not that to which my reason is inferior, but that to which nothing is superior.

AUGUSTINE: You're quite right, for God himself has enabled your reason to think so piously and correctly about him. But if you found nothing above our reason except what is eternal and unchangeable, would you hesitate to call that 'God'? For you know that material objects are changeable. It is obvious that the life by which the body is animated changes from one condition to another. And reason itself is clearly changeable: sometimes it strives for the truth and sometimes it doesn't; sometimes it attains the truth and sometimes it doesn't. If reason—not by any physical organ, not by touch or taste or smell, not by the ears or eyes or any sense inferior to itself, but by itself alone—sees something eternal and unchangeable, then it should confess that it is inferior, and that the eternal and unchangeable thing is its God.

EVODIUS: If we find that to which nothing is superior, I will certainly confess that it is God.

AUGUSTINE: Good. Then it will be enough for me to show that something of this sort exists, which you can admit to be God; or if something yet higher exists, you will concede that *it* is God. Therefore, whether there is something higher or not, it will be manifest that God exists, when I with his help fulfill my promise to prove that there is something higher than reason.

EVODIUS: Then show me your proof.

AUGUSTINE: I shall. But first I ask whether my bodily sense is the 7. same as yours, or whether mine and yours are distinct. If they were not distinct, I could not see anything that you didn't see.

EVODIUS: I quite agree. We have the same *sort* of senses, but we each have our own individual sense of sight and hearing and so on. Not only can one person *see* what another does not, but the same is true of hearing and each of the other senses. This clearly shows that my sense is distinct from your sense.

AUGUSTINE: Would you say the same thing about the inner sense?

EVODIUS: Of course. My inner sense perceives my sense; yours perceives your sense. Other people often ask me whether I see what they see, precisely because they do not perceive, as I do, whether I see it or not.

AUGUSTINE: Then what about reason? Doesn't each of us have his own reason? For it sometimes happens that I understand something that you don't understand. And you can't know whether I understand it, whereas I do know that I understand it.

EVODIUS: Clearly each of us possesses a distinct rational mind.

AUGUSTINE: Now each of us has his own sense of sight. But surely you wouldn't say that each of us has a private sun that he alone sees, or personal moons and stars and things of that sort.

EVODIUS: Of course not.

AUGUSTINE: Then many of us can see a single thing at the same time, although each of us sees it with his own individual sense. Thus, although your sense is distinct from my sense, it can happen that what you see is not distinct from what I see, but is a single thing that is present to both of us and is seen by both of us at once.

EVODIUS: That is quite obvious.

AUGUSTINE: We can also both hear the same sound at the same time. Thus, although my sense of hearing is distinct from yours, we do not hear two distinct sounds at the same time, and we do not each hear just part of the sound. Rather, there is one sound that is present as a whole to both of us at the same time.

EVODIUS: That is obvious too.

AUGUSTINE: You will notice that in this respect the other bodily senses are not quite the same as sight and hearing, but they are not totally dissimilar either. You and I can both breathe the same air and perceive its odor, and in the same way we can both taste the same honey, or some other food or drink, and perceive its flavor. Although there is only one object of perception, we both have our own separate and distinct senses. Thus, when we both perceive one odor and one flavor, you do not perceive with my sense nor I with yours. And we do not share one sense between us; I have mine and you have yours, even if we are both perceiving the same odor or flavor. So in this respect taste and smell are like sight and hearing.

But in another respect they are quite different. Even if we smell the same air or taste the same food, I do not inhale the same part of the air or eat the same part of the food as you. Of the total quantity of air, I breathe in one part that is enough for me, and you breathe in another part that is enough for you. And although we both partake of the same total quantity of food, we cannot both eat all of it, in the way that we can both hear all of the same word or see all of the same form at the same time. In the case of food or drink one part must enter my body and another part must enter yours. Do you understand this somewhat?

EVODIUS: Actually, I agree that this is quite straightforward and certain.

AUGUSTINE: Surely you don't think that the sense of touch is like sight or hearing in this respect. Not only can we both touch one object, but you can touch the very same part that I touched. Thus, by the sense of touch we can both perceive not only the same object, but the same *part* of the object. We cannot take the same quantity of food and both eat all of it, but this is not true of the sense of touch: you can touch all of what I touched. Thus, we need not confine ourselves to touching separate parts of an object; we can both touch all of it.

EVODIUS: In this respect, I admit, the sense of touch is quite similar to sight and hearing. But I see one difference. We can both see or hear all of something at the same time; but we can only touch different parts of something at the same time, or the same part of something at different times. For if you are touching something, I cannot touch it until you cease to touch it.

AUGUSTINE: A very astute reply. But notice this: there are, as we have seen, some objects of perception that both of us perceive, and some that we perceive individually. But we perceive our own senses individually—I don't perceive yours and you don't perceive mine. Now as for the things that we perceive by our bodily senses—that is, material objects—those that we must perceive individually are precisely those that we take and transform into a part of ourselves. Food and drink are like this: you can't taste any part that I have already tasted. Nurses give young children food that has already been chewed, but the part that has already been tasted and digested by the one who chewed it can in no way be recalled and used as food for the child. When the palate tastes something pleasant, however small, it claims that thing as an irrevocable part of itself and forces it to conform to the nature of the body. If this were not so, no taste would remain in the mouth after the food had been chewed and spat out.

The same is true of the parts of the air that we inhale through the nose. Doctors teach that we take in nourishment through the nose. But even if you can inhale some of the air that I exhale, you can't inhale the part that nourished me, because it must remain within me. Only I can inhale that nourishment, and I cannot exhale it and give it back for you to breathe.

There are other objects of perception that we perceive without transforming them into parts of our body and thereby destroying them. These are the things that both of us can perceive, either at the same time or at different times, in such a way that both of us perceive the whole object or the same part of the object. Among such things are light, sound, and any material object that we touch but leave intact.

EVODIUS: I understand.

AUGUSTINE: Then it is clear that the things we perceive but don't transform do not belong to the nature of our senses, and so we have them in common, since they do not become our own private property, as it were.

EVODIUS: I quite agree.

AUGUSTINE: By 'our own private property' I mean whatever belongs to us individually, that which is perceived by only one of us and belongs to the individual's own nature. By 'common and public property' I mean whatever can be perceived by everyone without any change or transformation.

EVODIUS: Agreed.

8. AUGUSTINE: Well then, tell me this. Can you think of anything that is common to all who think? I mean something that they all see with their own reason or mind, that is present to all but is not converted to the private use of those to whom it is present, as food and drink are, that remains unchanged and intact whether they see it or not? Or do you perhaps think that nothing like this exists?

EVODIUS: Actually, I see that there are many such things, but it will suffice to mention just one. The order and truth of number is present to all who think, so that those who make calculations try to grasp it by their own reason and understanding. Some can grasp it more easily than others can, but it offers itself equally to all who are capable of grasping it; unlike food, it is not transformed into a part of the one who perceives it. It is not at fault when someone makes a mistake; it remains true and complete, but the less one sees it, the greater is one's mistake.

AUGUSTINE: Quite right. Your quick reply shows that you are well acquainted with this subject. But suppose that someone told you that numbers are like images of visible things, that they are stamped on the soul, not by their own nature, but by the things that we perceive by the bodily senses. How would you respond? Would you agree?

EVODIUS: Not at all. Even if numbers were perceived by the bodily senses, it would not follow that I could also perceive the rules of addition and subtraction by the bodily senses. It is by the light of the mind that I refute someone who makes a mistake in adding or subtracting. Moreover, when I perceive something with the bodily sense, such as the earth and sky and the other material objects that I perceive in them, I don't know how much longer they are going to exist. But I do know that seven plus three equals ten, not just now, but always; it never has been and never will be the case that seven plus three does not equal ten. I therefore said that this incorruptible truth of number is common to me and all who think.

AUGUSTINE: Your reply is perfectly true and quite certain, so I make no objection. But you will easily see that numbers are not perceived by the bodily senses if you notice that each number is named on the basis of how many times it contains one. For example, if it contains one twice, it is called 'two', if three times, 'three', and if ten times, 'ten'. For any number at all, its name will be the number of times that it contains one. But anyone who thinks correctly will surely find that one cannot be perceived by the bodily senses. Anything that is perceived by such a sense is clearly not one but many, for it is a material object and therefore has countless parts. I won't even go into the minute and less complex parts, for any material object, however small, surely has a right and a left, a top and a bottom, a near side and a farther side, ends and a middle. We must admit that these parts are present in any material object, however tiny, and so we must concede that no material object is truly and simply one. And yet we could not enumerate so many parts unless we had some knowledge of what one is. For if I look for one in material objects and know that I have not found it, I must surely know what I was looking for and what I did not find there; indeed, I must know that it cannot be found there, or rather, that it is not there at all. And yet, if I did not know one, I could not distinguish many parts in material objects. So where did I come to know this *one* that is not a material object? Wherever it was, I did not come to know it through the bodily senses; the only things we know through the bodily senses are material objects, which we have found are not truly and simply one. Moreover, if we do not perceive *one* by the bodily sense, then we do not perceive *any number* by that sense, at least of those numbers that we grasp by the understanding. For every single one of them gets its name from the number of times that it contains one, which is not perceived by the bodily sense. The two halves of any material object together constitute the whole, but each half can in turn be divided in half. Thus, those two parts are in the object, but they are not strictly speaking two. But the number that is called 'two' contains twice that which is strictly speaking one. Thus, its half—that which is strictly speaking one—cannot be further subdivided, because it is simply and truly *one*.

After one comes two, which is two times one; but it does not follow that after two comes two times two. The next number is three, and then comes four, which is two times two. This order extends to all numbers by a fixed and unchangeable law. Thus, the first number after one (which is the first of all numbers) is two, which is two times one. The second number after two (which is the second number) is two times two—since the first number after two is three and the second number is four, which is two times two. The third number after three (which is the third number) is two times three—since the first number after three is four, the second number is five, and the third number is six, which is two times three. And the fourth number after the fourth number is twice that number; for the first number after four (which is the fourth number) is five, the second number is six, the third number is seven, and the fourth number is eight, which is two times four. And in all the rest you will find the same order that we found in the first two: however far any number is from the beginning, its double is in turn that far after it.

So we see that this order is fixed, secure, and unchangeable for all numbers. But how do we see this? No one perceives all the numbers by any bodily sense, for there are infinitely many of them. So where did we learn that this order extends to all of them? By what image or phantasm do we see so confidently this indisputable truth about number, which extends through infinitely many numbers? We see it by an inner light of which the bodily sense knows nothing.

For those inquirers to whom God has given the ability, whose judgment is not clouded by stubbornness, these and many other such examples suffice to show that the order and truth of numbers has nothing to do with the senses of the body, but that it does exist, complete and immutable, and can be seen in common by everyone who uses reason. Now there are many other things that are present generally and publicly, as it were, to those who use reason, and these things remain inviolate and unchangeable even though they are perceived separately by the mind and reason of each person who perceives them. Nonetheless, I do not object to the fact that the order and truth of number struck you most forcibly when you undertook to answer my question. It is no accident that Scripture associates number with wisdom: "I went around, I and my heart, that I might know and consider and seek after wisdom and number."[5]

5. Ecclesiastes 7:25

But then how do you think we ought to regard wisdom itself? **9.**
Do you think that each human being has his own personal wisdom? Or, on the contrary, is there one single wisdom that is
universally present to everyone, so that the more one partakes
of this wisdom, the wiser one is?

EVODIUS: I am not yet altogether certain what you mean by 'wisdom', since I see that people have different views about what
counts as wise in speech or action. Those who serve in wars think
that they are acting wisely. Those who despise the military and
devote their care and labor to farming think more highly of what
they do, and call it wise. Those who are clever in thinking up
money-making schemes consider themselves wise. Those who
neglect or renounce all of this, and everything that is temporal,
and devote all of their energy to searching for the truth so that
they might come to know themselves and God, judge that their
own actions are truly wise. Those who do not wish to give themselves up to the leisure of seeking and contemplating the truth
but instead busy themselves with the tedious duties of looking
after the interests of human beings, and work to ensure that
human affairs are justly regulated and governed, think that they
are wise. And then again, those who do both, who spend some
of their time in contemplating the truth and some of their time
in the tedious duties that they think are owed to human society,
regard themselves as the winners in the competition for wisdom.
I won't even mention the countless sects, each of which holds
that its own adherents are superior to everyone else, and that
they alone are wise. Therefore, since we have agreed to answer
only on the basis of what we clearly know, and not on the basis
of what we merely believe, I cannot answer your question unless,
in addition to believing, I know by reason and reflection what
wisdom is.

AUGUSTINE: But don't you think that wisdom is nothing other than
the truth in which the highest good is discerned and acquired? All
the different groups you mentioned seek good and shun evil;
what divides them is that each has a different opinion about what
is good. So whoever seeks what ought not to be sought is in error,
even though he would not seek it unless he thought it was good.
On the other hand, those who seek nothing at all, or who seek
what they ought to seek, cannot be in error. Therefore, insofar as
all human beings seek a happy life, they are not in error; but
to the extent that someone strays from the path that leads to

happiness—all the while insisting that his only goal is to be happy—to that extent he is in error, for 'error' simply means following something that doesn't take us where we want to go.[6]

Now the more one strays from the right path in life, the less wise one is, and so the further one is from the truth in which the highest good is discerned and acquired. But when one follows and attains the highest good, one becomes happy; and that, as we all agree, is precisely what we want. And so, just as it is obvious that we all want to be happy, it is also obvious that we all want to be wise, since no one can be happy without wisdom. For no one is happy without the highest good, which is discerned and acquired in the truth that we call 'wisdom'. Therefore, just as there is a notion of happiness stamped on our minds even before we are happy—for by means of that notion we know confidently and say without hesitation that we want to be happy—so we have the notion of wisdom stamped on our minds even before we are wise. By means of that notion all of us, if asked whether we want to be wise, answer yes, without the slightest hesitation.

Now that we have agreed about what wisdom is, although perhaps you could not explain it in words (for if your soul could not perceive wisdom at all, you would have no way of knowing both that you will to be wise and that you ought to will this, which I feel sure you won't deny), I want you to tell me whether wisdom, like the order and truth of number, is a single thing that presents itself to all who think; or rather, just as there are as many minds as there are human beings, so that I can see nothing of your mind and you can see nothing of mine, so there are as many wisdoms as there are potentially wise persons.

EVODIUS: If the highest good is one thing for everyone, then the truth in which that good is discerned and acquired must also be one thing that is common to all.

AUGUSTINE: But do you doubt that the highest good, whatever it is, is one thing for all human beings?

EVODIUS: Yes I do, because I see that different people take joy in different things as their highest good.

---

6. The root meaning of the Latin word *errare* is 'to stray from one's path, to lose one's way', but it was commonly extended to include moral and intellectual error.

AUGUSTINE: I only wish that people were as certain about what the highest good is as they are about the fact that human beings cannot be happy unless they attain it. But that is a great question and might require a long discussion, so let's assume that there are as many different highest goods as there are different things that various people seek as their highest good. Surely it does not follow from that assumption that wisdom itself is not one and common to all, simply because the goods that human beings discern and choose in it are many and various. That would be like thinking that there must be more than one sun, simply because we perceive many and various things by its light. What in fact happens is that each person uses the will to choose which of these many things to enjoy looking at. One person prefers to look upon the height of a mountain, and rejoices at the sight, while another chooses the flatness of a plain, another the hollow of a valley, another the verdure of a forest, another the pulsing tranquility of the sea, and another uses some or all of these at once to contribute to his pleasure in seeing. And so there are many and various things that human beings see in the light of the sun and choose for their enjoyment, even though the light itself is a single thing in which each person's gaze sees and pursues what he will enjoy. So even supposing that there are many and various goods from which each person chooses what he wants, and that by seeing and pursuing that thing he rightly and truly constitutes it his highest good, it is still possible that the light of wisdom, in which those things can be seen and pursued, is a single thing, common to all the wise.

EVODIUS: I admit that it is *possible*; there's no reason why wisdom can't be a single thing common to all, even if there are many diverse highest goods. But I would like to know whether it is really so. Just because we admit that it's possible, we can't conclude that it is in fact the case.

AUGUSTINE: So, for the time being at least, we hold that wisdom exists; but we don't yet know whether it is a single thing that is common to all, or whether each wise person has his own wisdom, just as he has his own soul and his own mind.

EVODIUS: Exactly.

AUGUSTINE: So we are agreed that wisdom exists, or at least that **10.** wise people exist, and that all human beings want to be happy. But *where* do we see this truth? For I have no doubt that you do see it, or that it is in fact true. Do you see this truth in the same way that you see your own thoughts, of which I am completely unaware unless you tell me about them? Or can I see it too, just as you understand it, even if I hear nothing about it from you?

EVODIUS: Clearly, you can see it too, even if I don't want you to.

AUGUSTINE: So this one truth, which each of us sees with his own mind, is common to both of us.

EVODIUS: Obviously.

AUGUSTINE: By the same token, I don't think you will deny that wisdom should be diligently sought after, and that this statement is in fact true.

EVODIUS: I am quite sure of that.

AUGUSTINE: Then this truth is a single truth that can be seen in common by all who know it. Nonetheless, each person sees it with his own mind—not with yours or mine or anyone else's—even though the truth that is seen is present in common to everyone who sees it.

EVODIUS: Exactly.

AUGUSTINE: Consider the following truths: one ought to live justly; inferior things should be subjected to superior things; like should be compared with like; everyone should be given what is rightly his. Don't you agree that these are true, and that they are present in common to me and you and all who see them?

EVODIUS: Yes.

AUGUSTINE: And you surely could not deny that the uncorrupted is better than the corrupt, the eternal than the temporal, and the invulnerable than the vulnerable.

EVODIUS: Could anyone?

AUGUSTINE: Can anyone say that this truth is his own private possession, given that it is unchangeably present to be contemplated by all who are able to contemplate it?

EVODIUS: No one could rightly say that it is his own, since it is as much one and common to all as it is true.

AUGUSTINE: Again, who would deny that one should turn one's soul from corruption to incorruption; or in other words, that one should not love corruption but rather incorruption? And who, admitting that this is true, would not also understand that this truth is unchangeable and see that it is present in common to every mind that is capable of perceiving it?

EVODIUS: You're quite right.

AUGUSTINE: And does anyone doubt that a life that cannot be swayed by any adversity from its fixed and upright resolve is better than one that is easily weakened and overthrown by transitory misfortunes?

EVODIUS: Who could doubt that?

AUGUSTINE: Then I won't look for more truths of this sort. It is enough that you too understand and concede that it is most certain that these rules, these lights of the virtues, are both true and unchangeable, and that they are present, either individually or collectively, to those who are able to see and contemplate them with their own mind and reason. But of course I must now ask whether you think that these truths are a part of wisdom. I'm sure you think that those who have attained wisdom are wise.

EVODIUS: Of course.

AUGUSTINE: Then consider those who live justly. Could they live thus unless they saw which inferior things to subject to which superior things, which like things to join to which, and which things to distribute to their rightful owners?

EVODIUS: No.

AUGUSTINE: And surely you will agree that someone who sees these things sees wisely.

EVODIUS: Yes.

AUGUSTINE: Now consider those who live in accordance with prudence. Do they not choose incorruption and recognize that it is to be preferred to corruption?

EVODIUS: Obviously.

AUGUSTINE: So when they choose the very thing that everyone admits they ought to choose, and turn their souls toward it, can it be denied that they choose wisely?

EVODIUS: I would certainly not deny it.

AUGUSTINE: So when they turn their souls toward that which they have wisely chosen, they are certainly turning them wisely.

EVODIUS: Absolutely.

AUGUSTINE: And those who are not deterred by any fear or punishment from that which they have wisely chosen, and toward which they have wisely turned, are undoubtedly acting wisely.

EVODIUS: Undoubtedly.

AUGUSTINE: Then it is utterly obvious that all of these truths that we called "rules" and "lights of the virtues" are part of wisdom, since the more one follows them and leads one's life by them, the more one lives and acts wisely. And whatever is done wisely cannot rightly be considered separate from wisdom.

EVODIUS: Exactly.

AUGUSTINE: So, just as there are true and unchangeable rules of numbers, whose order and truth you said are present unchangeably and in common to everyone who sees them, there are also true and unchangeable rules of wisdom. When I asked you about a few of these rules one by one, you replied that they are true and obvious, and you conceded that they are present in common to be contemplated by all who are capable of seeing them.

11. EVODIUS: I am quite certain of that. But I would very much like to know whether wisdom and number are both included in one single class. For as you have pointed out, wisdom and number are associated with each other even in Holy Scripture. Or perhaps one derives from the other or is contained in the other; for example, perhaps number derives from wisdom or is contained in wisdom. I wouldn't dream of saying that wisdom is derived from number or is contained in number. I don't know how that could be, for I have certainly known my share of mathematicians (or whatever you call those who are highly skilled at computation), but I have known very few who are wise— perhaps none at all—and wisdom strikes me as being far nobler than number.

AUGUSTINE: You have touched on a point that often astonishes me as well. For when I contemplate within myself the unchangeable truth of numbers and their lair (so to speak) and inner sanctuary or realm—or whatever else we might call their dwelling-place and home—I am far removed from material objects. I may, perhaps, find something that I can think about, but nothing that I can express in words. So in order to be able to say anything at all, I return in fatigue to familiar things and talk in the customary way about what is right in front of me. The same thing happens to me when I think as carefully and intently as I can about wisdom. So, given the fact that both wisdom and number are contained in that most hidden and certain truth, and that Scripture bears witness that the two are joined together, I very much wonder why most people consider wisdom valuable but have little respect for number. They are of course one and the same thing. Nevertheless, Scripture says of wisdom that "it reaches from end to end mightily and disposes all things sweetly."[7] Perhaps the power that "reaches from end to end mightily" is number, and the power that "disposes all things sweetly" is wisdom in the strict sense, although both powers belong to one and the same wisdom.

Every material object, however mean, has its numbers; but wisdom was granted, not to material objects or even to all souls, but only to rational souls, as if it set up in them a throne from which to dispose all the things, however lowly, to which it gave numbers. But wisdom gave numbers to everything, even to the lowliest and most far-flung things. Thus, since we perceive the numbers that are stamped upon them, we can easily make judgments about material objects as things ordered lower than ourselves. Consequently, we come to think that numbers themselves are also lower than we are, and we hold them in low esteem. But when we begin to look above ourselves again, we find that numbers transcend our minds and remain fixed in the truth itself. And since few can be wise, but even fools can count, people marvel at wisdom but disparage number. But the learned and studious, as they separate themselves more and more from earthly filth, come to see ever more clearly that wisdom and number are united in the truth itself, and they regard both as precious. In comparison with that truth, they consider everything else worthless—not just the silver and gold that human beings covet, but their very selves.

It should not surprise you that people honor wisdom and denigrate numbers, simply because it is easier to count than to be wise. For you see that they consider gold more precious than lamplight—and yet, in comparison with light, gold is a ridiculous trifle. People give greater honor to what is vastly inferior, simply because even a beggar has a lamp to light, while few have gold. I don't mean to imply that wisdom is inferior to number, for they are the same thing; but one needs an eye that can perceive that fact. Consider this analogy: light and heat are both perceived consubstantially, as it were, in the same fire; they cannot be separated from each other. Yet the heat affects only the things that are nearby, while the light is radiated far and wide. In the same

7. Wisdom 8:1

way, the power of understanding that inheres in wisdom warms the things that are closest to it, such as rational souls; whereas things that are further off, such as material objects, are not touched by the heat of wisdom, but they are flooded with the light of numbers. This matter may still be unclear to you; after all, no visible image can be perfectly analogous to something invisible. Nonetheless, you should notice this one point, which will suffice to answer the question that we set out to consider, and which is obvious even to lowly minds like ours. Even if we cannot be certain whether number is a part of wisdom or is derived from wisdom, or whether wisdom itself is a part of number or is derived from number, or whether both are names for a single thing, it is certainly clear that both are true, and indeed unchangeably true.

12.   So you cannot deny the existence of an unchangeable truth that contains everything that is unchangeably true. And you cannot claim that this truth is yours or mine or anyone else's; it is present and reveals itself in common to all who discern what is unchangeably true, like a light that is public and yet strangely hidden. But if it is present in common to all who reason and understand, who could think that it belongs exclusively to the nature of any one of them? I'm sure you remember what we discussed earlier about the bodily senses. The things that we perceive in common by the sense of the eyes and ears, such as colors and sounds that both of us see or hear, do not belong to the nature of our eyes or ears; rather, they are present in common for both of us to perceive. So you would never say that the things that you and I both perceive, each with his own mind, belong to the nature of my mind or of yours. When two people see the same thing with their eyes, you cannot say that they are seeing the eyes of one or the other of them, but some third thing at which both of them are looking.

EVODIUS: That is quite obviously true.

AUGUSTINE: Well then, what do you think of this truth we have been discussing for so long, in which we see so many things? Is it more excellent than our minds, or equal to them, or even inferior to them? If it were inferior, we would make judgments *about* it, not *in accordance with* it, just as we make judgments about material objects because they are below us. We often say, not just that they *are* a certain way, but that they *ought to be* that way. The same is true of our souls: we often know, not merely that they *are* a certain way, but that they *ought to be* that way. We make such judgments about material objects when we say that something is not as white as it ought to be, or not as square, and so on. But we say that a soul is less capable than it ought to be, or less gentle, or less forceful, depending on our own character. We make these judgments *in accordance with* the inner rules of truth, which we perceive in common; but no one makes judgments *about* those rules. When someone says that eternal things are better than temporal things, or that seven plus three equals ten, no one says that it ought to be so. We simply recognize that it is so; we are like explorers who rejoice in what they have discovered, not like inspectors who have to put things right.

Furthermore, if this truth were equal to our minds, it too would be changeable. For our minds see the truth better at some times than at others, which shows that they are indeed changeable. But the truth makes no progress when we see it better and suffers no setback when we see it less. It remains whole and undefiled, giving the joy of its light to those who turn toward it but inflicting blindness on those who turn away. Why, we even make judgments about our own minds in accordance with that truth, while we can in no way make judgments about it. We say that a mind does not understand as much as it ought to, or that it understands just as much as it ought to. And the more a mind can be turned toward the unchangeable truth and cleave to it, the more it ought to understand.

Therefore, since the truth is neither inferior nor equal to our minds, we can conclude that it is superior to them and more excellent than they are.

But I had promised, if you recall, that I would prove that there **13.** is something more sublime than our mind and reason. Here it is: the truth itself. Embrace it, if you can; enjoy it; "delight in the Lord, and he will give you the desires of your heart."[8] What more can you desire than happiness? And what greater happiness can there be than to enjoy the unshakable, unchangeable, and most excellent truth?

People cry out that they are happy when they passionately embrace the beautiful bodies of their spouses, and even of prostitutes; and shall we doubt that we are happy in embracing the

8. Psalm 37:4

truth? People cry out that they are happy when, with throats parched by the heat, they come upon a wholesome and abundant spring, or when they are starving and find an elaborate feast; and shall we deny that we are happy when our thirst is quenched and our hunger appeased by the truth itself? We often hear voices crying out that they are happy if they lie among roses or other flowers, or enjoy the incomparable scent of the finest perfumes; what is more fragrant, more delightful, than the gentle breath of truth? And shall we doubt that we are happy when it breathes upon us? Many find their happiness in the music of voices and strings and flutes. When they are without it, they think they are miserable; and when they have it, they are in raptures. So when the silent eloquence of truth flows over us without the clamor of voices, shall we look for some other happiness, and not enjoy the one that is so secure and so near at hand? People take pleasure in the cheerfulness and brightness of light—in the glitter of gold and silver, in the brilliance of gems, and in the radiance of colors and of that very light that belongs to our eyes, whether in earthly fires or in the stars or the sun or the moon. As long as no poverty or violence deprives them of this joy, they think that they are happy; they want to live forever to enjoy such a happiness. And shall we fear to find our happiness in the light of truth?

No! Rather, since the highest good is known and acquired in the truth, and that truth is wisdom, let us enjoy to the full the highest good, which we see and acquire in that truth. For those who enjoy the highest good are happy indeed. This truth shows forth all good things that are true, holding them out to be grasped by whoever has understanding and chooses one or many of them for his enjoyment. Now think for a moment of those who choose what pleases them in the light of the sun and take joy in gazing upon it. If only their eyes were livelier and sound and exceptionally strong, they would like nothing better than to look directly upon the sun, which sheds its light even on the inferior things that weaker eyes delight in. It is just the same with a strong and lively mind. Once it has contemplated many true and unchangeable things with the sure eye of reason, it turns to the truth itself, by which all those true things are made known. It forgets those other things and cleaves to the truth, in which it enjoys them all at once. For whatever is delightful in the other true things is especially delightful in the truth itself.

This is our freedom, when we are subject to the truth; and the truth is God himself, who frees us from death, that is, from the state of sin. For that truth, speaking as a human being to those who believe in him, says, "If you abide in my word, you are truly my disciples. And you shall know the truth, and the truth shall make you free."[9] For the soul enjoys nothing with freedom unless it enjoys it securely.

Now no one is secure in enjoying goods that can be lost against **14.** his will. But no one can lose truth and wisdom against his will, for no one can be separated from the place where they are. What we called separation from truth and wisdom is really just a perverse will that loves inferior things, and no one wills something unwillingly. We can all enjoy it equally and in common; there is ample room, and it lacks for nothing. It welcomes all of its lovers without envy; it belongs to them all but is faithful to each. No one says to another, "Step back so that I too can get close; let go of it so that I too can embrace it." They all cleave to it; they all touch it. No one tears off a piece as his own food; you drink nothing from it that I cannot also drink. For what you gain from that communion does not become your own private property; it remains intact for me. When you breathe it in, I need not wait for you to give it back so that I can breathe it too. No part of it ever becomes the private property of any one person; it is always wholly present to everyone.

Therefore, the things that we touch or taste or smell are less similar to this truth than are the things that we hear and see. For every word that is heard is heard simultaneously and in its entirety by everyone who hears it, and any form that is seen by the eyes is seen equally by every eye that sees it. But these things bear only a very distant resemblance to the truth. For no sound exists all at once; every sound is produced in time and is distended in time, and one part of it is heard after another. And every visible form is extended in place and does not exist as a whole in any one place.

Moreover, any of these things can surely be taken away from us against our will, and there are many obstacles that keep us from enjoying them fully. For example, even if someone could

9. John 8:31–32

sing a beautiful song that never came to an end, and those who were keen on it came eagerly to hear it, they would crowd together and fight for the places nearest the singer. And even then, they could not hold on forever to what they heard; the sounds would reach them and then vanish. Even if I wanted to look at the sun and could do so with an unflinching eye, it would desert me at sunset or when it was hidden by a cloud; and many other things would interfere with my pleasure in seeing the sun, and so I would lose it against my will. Besides, even supposing that I could always see a brilliant light or hear a beautiful sound, what would that profit me? I would have that in common with beasts.

But to the will that steadfastly desires to enjoy it, the beauty of truth and wisdom is not obscured by the crowds of eager listeners. It is not used up in the course of time; it does not move from place to place. Night does not cover it, and no shadow hides it. The bodily senses do not perceive it. It is near to those in all the world who turn themselves toward it and love it. It is eternally present with them all. It is not in any place, but it is present everywhere. It warns outwardly and teaches inwardly. It changes for the better all those who see it, and no one changes it for the worse. No one judges it, but apart from it no one judges rightly. And so it is clear beyond any doubt that this one truth, by which people become wise, and which makes them judges, not of it, but of other things, is better than our minds.

15.   Now you had conceded that if I proved the existence of something higher than our minds, you would admit that it was God, as long as there was nothing higher still. I accepted this concession, and said that it would be enough if I proved that there is something higher than our minds. For if there is something more excellent than the truth, then that is God; if not, the truth itself is God. So in either case you cannot deny that God exists, and that was the very question that we had agreed to discuss. Perhaps it occurs to you that, according to the teaching of Christ that we have accepted in faith, Wisdom has a Father.[10] But remember another thing that we have accepted in faith: the Wisdom that is begotten of the eternal Father is equal to him. That is not a matter

---

10. Augustine is alluding to the common practice of referring to God the Son as "Wisdom." Cf. 1 Corinthians 1:24: "Christ the Power of God and the Wisdom of God."

for dispute right now; we must hold it with unshaken faith. For there is indeed a God, and he exists truly and in the highest degree. No longer is this a truth that we merely hold with unhesitating faith; we have achieved an unerring, although extremely superficial, form of knowledge. This is enough to enable us to explain the other things that relate to our question, unless you have some objection to make.

EVODIUS: I am so overwhelmed with joy that I cannot express it in words. I accept what you say; indeed, I cry out that it is most certain. But I cry out inwardly, hoping to be heard by the truth itself and to cleave to it. For I recognize that it is not merely one good among others; it is the highest good, the good that makes us happy.

AUGUSTINE: You do well to feel such joy—I too am rejoicing greatly. But I ask you, are we already happy and wise? Or are we merely on our way?

EVODIUS: I think we are merely on our way.

AUGUSTINE: Then how do you understand these certain truths that make you cry out for joy? And how do you know that they belong to wisdom? Can a fool know wisdom?

EVODIUS: Not as long as he remains a fool.

AUGUSTINE: So either you are wise, or you do not yet know wisdom.

EVODIUS: I'm not yet wise, but I wouldn't say that I am a fool either, since I do know wisdom. For I can't deny that the things I know are certain or that they belong to wisdom.

AUGUSTINE: But Evodius, wouldn't you agree that someone who is not just is unjust, and someone who is not prudent is imprudent, and someone who is not temperate is intemperate? Or is there some room for doubt on these matters?

EVODIUS: I agree that when someone is not just he is unjust; and I would say the same thing about prudence and temperance.

AUGUSTINE: So when someone is not wise, isn't he a fool?[11]

EVODIUS: Yes, I agree with that too. When someone is not wise he is a fool.

AUGUSTINE: Well then, which are you?

---

11. In Latin, the word for 'wise' (*sapiens*) is related to the word for 'fool' (*insipiens*) just as 'prudent' is to 'imprudent', 'temperate' to 'intemperate', and 'just' to 'unjust'.

Evodius: Call me whichever you like. I wouldn't dream of saying that I am wise, so given what I have just agreed to, I see that I must admit to being a fool.

Augustine: Then a fool knows wisdom. For as we said before, you could not be certain that you willed to be wise, and that you ought to do so, unless a notion of wisdom was present in your mind. The same is true of the things that you said in response to each of my questions, things that belong to wisdom itself and that you rejoiced to understand.

Evodius: Exactly.

16. Augustine: What then are we doing when we diligently strive to be wise? Do we not seek, with as much energy as we can command, to gather our whole soul somehow to that which we attain by the mind, to station ourselves and become firmly entrenched there, so that we may no longer rejoice in our own private goods, which are bound up with ephemeral things, but instead cast aside all attachments to times and places and apprehend that which is always one and the same? For just as the soul is the whole life of the body, so God is the happy life of the soul. While we are striving thus—as long as we do so wholeheartedly—we are on our way. We have been allowed to rejoice in these true and certain goods, even though for now they are like lightning flashes on this dark road. Isn't it written of Wisdom that she does this for her lovers when they come to her and seek her? For it is said, "She graciously reveals herself to them along the way, and in all of providence she runs to meet them."[12] Wherever you turn, she speaks to you in the traces that she leaves in her works. When you sink back down into external things, she uses the forms of those very things to call you back inside, so that you can see that whatever pleases you in material objects and entices you through the bodily senses has number. Thus you will ask where that number comes from; returning within yourself, you will understand that you could neither approve nor disapprove of anything you perceive through the bodily senses unless you had within yourself certain laws of beauty to which you refer every beautiful thing that you see outside yourself.

Consider the heavens and the earth and the sea and everything

12. Wisdom 6:16

in them that shines from on high or crawls here below, everything that flies or swims. They have forms because they have numbers; take away their form and number and they will be nothing. So they derive their being from the same source as number, for they have being only insofar as they have number.

Craftsmen who shape all kinds of physical forms use the numbers that they have in their craft to fashion their works. They put their hands and their tools to work until the object, which is being fashioned externally in accordance with the light of the mind within, is made as perfect as possible. The senses relay the object to the inner judge, which beholds the numbers above it, and it is pleased.

Next, ask what moves the craftsman's hands; it is number, for they too are moved in accordance with number. Now take away the work from his hands and the design from his mind, and imagine that he is moving his body for the sake of pleasure—you will call that "dancing." Ask what it is about dancing that gives pleasure: number will reply, "It is I."

Now consider the beauty of a material object at rest; its numbers remain in place. Consider the beauty of a material object in motion: its numbers vary through time. Enter into the craft from which these things proceed, and look in it for time and place: it exists at no time and in no place, for number dwells in it; its realm is not confined to space, nor is its age measured in days. When those who want to become craftsmen set themselves to learn the craft, they move their bodies in time and space, but their minds only in time; that is, they become more skilled with the passage of time.

Now pass beyond the mind of the craftsman to see eternal number. Wisdom itself will shine upon you from its inner throne and from the secret dwelling-place of truth. And if its brilliance overwhelms your weak sight, turn the eye of your mind back to the road on which wisdom revealed itself to you graciously. But remember that you have merely put off a vision that you will seek again when you are stronger and healthier.

O wisdom, the sweetest light of a purified mind! Woe to those who abandon you as their guide and ramble about where you have left your traces, who love the things in which you speak to us instead of loving you, and forget what you are telling us. For you do not cease to tell us what and how great you are, and you speak to us in the beauty of every created thing. Even a craftsman somehow speaks in the very beauty of his work to the one who sees it, bidding him not to devote all his attention to the appearance of the material object that has been produced, but to look beyond it and recall with affection the one who produced it. But those who love what you make instead of loving you are like people who hear someone speaking wisely and eloquently and listen keenly to the charm of his voice and the construction of his words, while ignoring the most important thing: the meaning that his words signified.

Woe to those who turn away from your light and gladly embrace a darkness of their own. They turn their backs on you and are bewitched by the works of the flesh, which are like their own shadows; and yet even then, the things that delight them have something of the radiance of your light. But when someone loves a shadow, the eye of the soul grows weaker and more inadequate to look upon you. So he wanders in darkness more and more, and gladly pursues whatever comes easiest to him in his weakened state. Soon he is unable to see what exists in the highest degree. He thinks it is evil when someone cheats him when he is off his guard, or defrauds him when he is in want, or takes him captive and tortures him. But he deservedly suffers these things because he has turned away from wisdom, and what is just cannot be evil.

Whatever changeable thing you may look at, you could not grasp it at all, either by the sense of the body or by the contemplation of the mind, unless it had some form composed of numbers, without which it would sink into nothing. Therefore, do not doubt that there is an eternal and unchangeable form that sees to it that these changeable things do not perish, but pass through time in measured motions and a distinct variety of forms, like the verses of a song. This eternal form has no bounds; although it is diffused everywhere, it is not extended in place, and it does not change in time. But through it all changeable things can be formed, and thus they complete and carry out the numbers of times and places in the way appropriate to things of their class.

17.   For every changeable thing is necessarily also formable. (Since we call something that can be changed "changeable," I shall call whatever can be formed "formable.") But nothing can form itself, since a thing can't give what it doesn't have. So if something is

to have a form, it must be formed by something else. If a thing already has some form, it has no need to receive what it already has; but if it lacks that form, it cannot receive from itself what it does not have. Therefore, as we said, nothing can form itself. And what more is there for us to say about the changeableness of both body and soul? Enough has already been said. And so it follows that both body and soul are formed by an unchangeable form that abides for ever.

To this form it has been said, "You will change them, and they shall be changed; but you are always the same, and your years will not fail."[13] By "years without fail" the prophet means "eternity." It is also said of this form that "abiding in himself he makes all things new."[14] From this we understand that everything is governed by his providence. For if everything that exists would be nothing without form, then that unchangeable form—through which all changeable things subsist, so that they complete and carry out the numbers of their forms—is itself the providence that governs them. For they would not exist if it did not exist. Therefore, whoever has contemplated the whole creation and considers it carefully, if he follows the way that leads to wisdom, will indeed see that wisdom reveals itself graciously to him along the way and that in all of providence it runs to meet him. And as the joy of his burning desire to follow that way grows stronger, the very wisdom that he so ardently longs to achieve will make his way more beautiful.

Now if you can manage to find some sort of creature beyond what has existence but not life, and what has existence and life but not understanding, and what has existence, life, and understanding, then you may dare to say that there is some good thing that is not from God. For these three classes may be designated by two words, 'matter' and 'life', since both that which has life but not understanding, such as the lower animals, and that which has understanding, like human beings, can quite properly be called 'life'. But these two things, considered as creatures—for the word 'life' is also applied to the Creator himself, and his life is life in the highest degree—these two creatures, matter and life,

13. Psalm 102:26–27
14. Wisdom 7:27

are formable, as our previous statements showed. And since if they lost their form altogether they would fall into nothingness, it is quite clear that they subsist from that form that is always the same. Therefore, there can be no good thing, however great or small, that is not from God. For what created things could be greater than a life that understands or less than matter? However much they may lack form, and however great may be their propensity not to exist, nonetheless some form remains in them so that they do exist in some way. And whatever form remains in a deficient thing comes from the form that knows no deficiency and does not allow the motions of growing or decaying things to transgress the laws of their own numbers. Therefore, whatever is found to be praiseworthy in nature, whether it is judged worthy of small praise or great, should be referred to the ineffable and most excellent praise of their maker. Or do you have some objection to make?

18. EVODIUS: I confess that I am quite convinced that this is the way to prove that God exists—as well as it can be proven in this life among people like us. And I am also convinced that all good things come from God, since everything that exists—whether that which has understanding, life, and existence, or that which has only life and existence, or that which has existence alone—is from God. Now let's take a look at the third question and see whether it can be resolved: should free will be included among those good things? Once that has been shown, I will concede without hesitation that God gave it to us, and that he was right to do so.
AUGUSTINE: You have done a good job of remembering what we set out to do, and you have most astutely realized that the second question has now been answered. But you ought to have seen that the third question too has already been answered. You had said that it seemed that God should not have given us free choice of the will, because whoever sins does so by free choice. I said in reply that no one can act rightly except by that same free choice of the will, and I affirmed that God gave us free choice in order to enable us to act rightly. You replied that free will should have been given to us in the same way that justice is given; no one can use justice wrongly. That reply of yours drove us into a roundabout path of discussion; along the way we showed that there is nothing good, however great or small, that is not from God. But that fact could not be shown clearly enough until we

had first challenged the irreligious stupidity of the fool who "said in his heart, 'There is no God'."[15] by attempting to find some evident truth to the contrary, going as far as our reason can take us in such an important matter, with God helping us along this precarious path. But these two facts—I mean that God exists and that every good thing is from him—which of course we believed quite confidently even before this discussion, have now been so thoroughly considered that this third fact seems altogether obvious: free will should indeed be counted as a good thing.

For earlier in our discussion it had become clear, and we had agreed, that the nature of the body is at a lower level than the nature of the soul, and so the soul is a greater good than the body. But even when we find good things in the body that we can use wrongly, we do not say that they ought not to have been given to the body, for we admit that they are in fact good. So why should it be surprising that there are also good things in the soul that we can use wrongly, but which, since they are in fact good, can only have been given by him from whom all good things come?

Consider what a great good a body is missing if it has no hands. And yet people use their hands wrongly in committing violent or shameful acts. If you see someone who has no feet, you admit that his physical well-being is impaired by the absence of so great a good, and yet you would not deny that someone who uses his feet to harm someone else or to disgrace himself is using them wrongly. By our eyes we see light and we distinguish the forms of material objects. They are the most beautiful thing in our bodies, so they were put into the place of greatest dignity; and we use them to preserve our safety and to secure many other good things in life. Nonetheless, many people use their eyes to do many evil things and press them into the service of inordinate desire; and yet you realize what a great good is missing in a face that has no eyes. But when they are present, who gave them, if not God, the generous giver of all good things? So just as you approve of these good things in the body and praise the one who gave them, disregarding those who use them wrongly, you should admit that free will, without which no one can live rightly, is a good

15. Psalm 14:1; 53:1

and divine gift. You should condemn those who misuse this good
rather than saying that he who gave it should not have given it.
EVODIUS: But first I would like for you to prove that free will is
a good thing, and then I will concede that God gave it to us, since
I admit that all good things come from God.
AUGUSTINE: But didn't I just go to a great deal of trouble to
prove that in our earlier discussion, when you admitted that every
species and form of every material object subsists from the highest
form of all things, that is, from truth, and when you conceded
that they are good? The truth itself tells us in the gospel that the
very hairs of our head are numbered.[16] Have you forgotten what
we said about the supremacy of number, and its power reaching
from end to end? What perversity, then, to number the hairs of
our head among the good things, though of course among the
least and most trivial goods, and to attribute them to God, the
creator of all good things—for both the greatest and the least
goods come from him from whom all good things come—and
yet to have doubts about free will, when even those who lead
the worst lives admit that no one can live rightly without it! Tell
me now, which is better: something without which we *can* live
rightly, or something without which we *cannot* live rightly?
EVODIUS: Please, stop; I am ashamed of my blindness. Who could
doubt that something without which no one lives rightly is far
superior?
AUGUSTINE: Would you deny that a one-eyed man can live rightly?
EVODIUS: That would be crazy.
AUGUSTINE: But you admit that an eye is something good in the
body, even though losing it does not interfere with living rightly.
So don't you think that free will is a good, since no one can live
rightly without it? Look at justice, which no one uses wrongly.
Justice, and indeed all the virtues of the soul, are counted among
the highest goods that are in human beings, because they constitute an upright and worthy life. For no one uses prudence or
fortitude or temperance wrongly; right reason, without which
they would not even be virtues, prevails in all of them, just as it
does in justice, which you mentioned. And no one can use right
reason wrongly.

16. Cf. Matthew 10:30

Therefore, these virtues are great goods. But you must remem- **19.**
ber that even the lowest goods can exist only from him from
whom all good things come, that is, from God. For that was
the conclusion of our previous discussion, which you so gladly
assented to many times. Thus, the virtues, by which one lives
rightly, are great goods; the beauty of various material objects,
without which one can live rightly, are the lowest goods; and the
powers of the soul, without which one cannot live rightly, are
intermediate goods. No one uses the virtues wrongly, but the
other goods, both the lowest and the intermediate, can be used
either rightly or wrongly. The virtues cannot be used wrongly
precisely because it is their function to make the right use of
things that can also be used wrongly, and no one uses something
wrongly by using it rightly. So the abundant generosity of the
goodness of God has bestowed not only the great goods, but also
the lowest and intermediate goods. His goodness deserves more
praise for the great goods than for the intermediate goods, and
more for the intermediate goods than for the lowest goods; but
it deserves more praise for creating all of them than it would
deserve for creating only some of them.

Evodius: I agree. But there is one thing that concerns me. We see
that it is free will that uses other things either rightly or wrongly.
So how can free will itself be included among the things that we
use?

Augustine: In the same way that we know by reason everything
that we know, and yet reason itself is included among the things
that we know by reason. Or have you forgotten that when we
were asking what we know by reason, you admitted that we
know reason itself by means of reason? So don't be surprised
that, even though we use other things by free will, we also use
free will itself by means of free will, so that the will that uses
other things also uses itself, just as the reason that knows other
things also knows itself. Similarly, memory not only grasps everything else that we remember, but also somehow retains itself in
us, since we do not forget that we have a memory. It remembers
not only other things but also itself; or rather, through memory
we remember not only other things, but also memory itself.

Therefore, when the will, which is an intermediate good, cleaves
to the unchangeable good that is common, not private—namely,
the truth, of which we have said much, but nothing adequate—

then one has a happy life. And the happy life, that is, the disposition of a soul that cleaves to the unchangeable good, is the proper and principal good for a human being. It contains all the virtues, which no one can use wrongly. Now the virtues, although they are great and indeed the foremost things in human beings, are not sufficiently common, since they belong exclusively to the individual human being who possesses them. But truth and wisdom are common to all, and all who are wise and happy become so by cleaving to truth and wisdom. No one becomes happy by someone else's happiness; even if you pattern yourself after someone else in order to become happy, your desire is to attain happiness from the same source as the other person, that is, from the unchangeable truth that is common to you both. No one becomes prudent by someone else's prudence, or resolute by someone else's fortitude, or temperate by someone else's temperance, or just by someone else's justice. Instead, you regulate your soul by those unchangeable rules and lights of the virtues that dwell incorruptibly in the common truth and wisdom, just as the one whose virtue you set out to imitate regulated his soul and fixed it upon those rules.

Therefore, when the will cleaves to the common and unchangeable good, it attains the great and foremost goods for human beings, even though the will itself is only an intermediate good. But when the will turns away from the unchangeable and common good toward its own private good, or toward external or inferior things, it sins. It turns toward its own private good when it wants to be under its own control; it turns toward external things when it is keen on things that belong to others or have nothing to do with itself; it turns toward inferior things when it takes delight in physical pleasure. In this way one becomes proud, meddlesome, and lustful; one is caught up into a life that, by comparison with the higher life, is death. But even that life is governed by divine providence, which places all things in their proper order and gives everyone what he deserves.

Hence, the goods that are pursued by sinners are in no way evil things, and neither is free will itself, which we found is to be counted among the intermediate goods. What is evil is the turning of the will away from the unchangeable good and toward changeable goods. And since this turning is not coerced, but voluntary, it is justly and deservedly punished with misery.

But perhaps you are going to ask what is the source of this **20.** movement by which the will turns away from the unchangeable good toward a changeable good. This movement is certainly evil, even though free will itself is to be counted among good things, since no one can live rightly without it. For if that movement, that turning away from the Lord God, is undoubtedly sin, surely we cannot say that God is the cause of sin. So that movement is not from God. But then where does it come from? If I told you that I don't know, you might be disappointed; but that would be the truth. For one cannot know that which is nothing.

You must simply hold with unshaken faith that every good thing that you perceive or understand or in any way know is from God. For any nature you come across is from God. So if you see anything at all that has measure, number, and order, do not hesitate to attribute it to God as craftsman. If you take away all measure, number, and order, there is absolutely nothing left. Even if the rudiments of a form remain, in which you find neither measure nor number nor order—since wherever those things are there is a complete form—you must take that away too, for it seems to be like the material on which the craftsman works. For if the completion of form is a good, then the rudiments of a form are themselves not without goodness. So if you take away everything that is good, you will have absolutely nothing left. But every good thing comes from God, so there is no nature that does not come from God. On the other hand, every defect comes from nothing, and that movement of turning away, which we admit is sin, is a defective movement. So you see where that movement comes from; you may be sure that it does not come from God.

But since that movement is voluntary, it has been placed under our control. If you fear it, do not will it; and if you do not will it, it will not exist. What greater security could there be than to have a life in which nothing can happen to you that you do not will? But since we cannot pick ourselves up voluntarily as we fell voluntarily, let us hold with confident faith the right hand of God—that is, our Lord Jesus Christ—which has been held out to us from on high. Let us await him with resolute hope and desire him with ardent charity. But if you think that we need to discuss the origin of sin more carefully, we must postpone that for another discussion.

EVODIUS: I will bow to your will and postpone this question, for I don't think that we have investigated it thoroughly enough yet.

Book Three

1. EVODIUS: It has been demonstrated to my satisfaction that free will is to be numbered among good things, and indeed not among the least of them, and therefore that it was given to us by God, who acted rightly in giving it. So now, if you think that this is a good time, I would like you to explain the source of the movement by which the will turns away from the common and unchangeable good toward its own good, or the good of others, or lower goods, all of which are changeable.

AUGUSTINE: Why do we need to know that?

EVODIUS: Because if the will was given to us in such a way that it had this movement naturally, then it turned to changeable goods by necessity, and there is no blame involved when nature and necessity determine an action.

AUGUSTINE: Does this movement please you or displease you?

EVODIUS: It displeases me.

AUGUSTINE: So you find fault with it.

EVODIUS: Of course.

AUGUSTINE: Then you find fault with a blameless movement of the soul.

EVODIUS: No, it's just that I don't know whether there is any blame involved when the soul deserts the unchangeable good and turns toward changeable goods.

AUGUSTINE: Then you find fault with what you don't know.

EVODIUS: Don't quibble over words. In saying "I don't know whether there is any blame involved," I meant it to be understood that there undoubtedly *is* blame involved. The "I don't know" implied that it was ridiculous to have doubts about such an obvious fact.

AUGUSTINE: Then pay close attention to this most certain truth, which has caused you to forget so quickly what you just said. If that movement existed by nature or necessity, it could in no way be blameworthy. But you are so firmly convinced that this movement is indeed blameworthy that you think it would be ridiculous to entertain doubts about something so certain. Why then did you affirm, or at least tentatively assert, something that now seems to you clearly false? For this is what you said: "If the will was given to us in such a way that it had this movement naturally, then it turned to changeable goods by necessity, and there is no blame involved when nature and necessity determine an action." Since you are sure that this movement was blameworthy, you should have been quite sure that the will was not given to us in such a way.

EVODIUS: I said that this movement was blameworthy and that therefore it displeases me. And I am surely right to find fault with it. But I deny that a soul ought to be blamed when this movement pulls it away from the unchangeable good toward changeable goods, if this movement is so much a part of its nature that it is moved by necessity.

AUGUSTINE: You admit that this movement certainly deserves blame; but *whose* movement is it?

EVODIUS: I see that the movement is in the soul, but I don't know whose it is.

AUGUSTINE: Surely you don't deny that the soul is moved by this movement.

EVODIUS: No.

AUGUSTINE: Do you deny that a movement by which a stone is moved is a movement of the stone? I'm not talking about a movement that is caused by us or some other force, as when it is thrown into the air, but the movement that occurs when it falls to the earth by its own weight.

EVODIUS: I don't deny that this movement, by which the stone seeks the lowest place, is a movement of the stone. But it is a natural movement. If that's the sort of movement the soul has, then the soul's movement is also natural. And if it is moved naturally, it cannot justly be blamed; even if it is moved toward something evil, it is compelled by its own nature. But since we don't doubt that this movement is blameworthy, we must absolutely deny that it is natural, and so it is not similar to the natural movement of a stone.

AUGUSTINE: Did we accomplish anything in our first two discussions?

EVODIUS: Of course we did.

AUGUSTINE: I'm sure you recall that in Book One we agreed that nothing can make the mind a slave to inordinate desire except its own will. For the will cannot be forced into such iniquity by anything superior or equal to it, since that would be unjust; or by anything inferior to it, since that is impossible. Only one possi-

bility remains: the movement by which the will turns from enjoying the Creator to enjoying his creatures belongs to the will itself.
So if that movement deserves blame (and you said it was ridiculous to entertain doubts on that score), then it is not natural, but
voluntary.

This movement of the will is similar to the downward movement of a stone in that it belongs to the will just as that downward
movement belongs to the stone. But the two movements are dissimilar in this respect: the stone has no power to check its downward movement, but the soul is not moved to abandon higher
things and love inferior things unless it wills to do so. And so
the movement of the stone is natural, but the movement of the
soul is voluntary. If someone were to say that a stone is sinning
because its weight carries it downward, I would not merely say
that he was more senseless than the stone itself; I would consider
him completely insane. But we accuse a soul of sin when we are
convinced that it has abandoned higher things and chosen to
enjoy inferior things. Now we admit that this movement belongs
to the will alone, and that it is voluntary and therefore blameworthy; and the only useful teaching on this topic is that which
condemns and checks this movement and thus serves to rescue
our wills from their fall into temporal goods and turn them toward
the enjoyment of the eternal good. Therefore, what need is there
to ask about the source of the movement by which the will turns
away from the unchangeable good toward changeable good?

EVODIUS: I see that what you are saying is true, and in a way I
understand it. There is nothing I feel so firmly and so intimately
as that I have a will by which I am moved to enjoy something.
If the will by which I choose or refuse things is not mine, then I
don't know what I can call mine. So if I use my will to do something evil, whom can I hold responsible but myself? For a good
God made me, and I can do nothing good except through my
will; therefore, it is quite clear that the will was given to me by
a good God so that I might do good. If the movement of the will
by which it turns this way or that were not voluntary and under
its own control, a person would not deserve praise for turning
to higher things or blame for turning to lower things, as if swing-
ing on the hinge of the will. Furthermore, there would be no
point in admonishing people to forget about lower things and
strive for what is eternal, so that they might refuse to live badly

but instead will to live rightly. And anyone who does not think that we ought to admonish people in this way deserves to be banished from the human race.

Since these things are true, I very much wonder how God can **2.** have foreknowledge of everything in the future, and yet we do not sin by necessity. It would be an irreligious and completely insane attack on God's foreknowledge to say that something could happen otherwise than as God foreknew. So suppose that God foreknew that the first human being was going to sin. Anyone who admits, as I do, that God foreknows everything in the future will have to grant me that. Now I won't say that God would not have made him—for God made him good, and no sin of his can harm God, who not only made him good but showed His own goodness by creating him, as He also shows His justice by punishing him and His mercy by redeeming him—but I will say this: since God foreknew that he was going to sin, his sin necessarily had to happen. How, then, is the will free when such inescapable necessity is found in it?

AUGUSTINE: You have knocked powerfully on the door of God's mercy; may it be present and open the door to those who knock. Nevertheless, I think the only reason that most people are tormented by this question is that they do not ask it piously; they are more eager to excuse than to confess their sins. Some people gladly believe that there is no divine providence in charge of human affairs. They put their bodies and their souls at the mercy of chance and give themselves up to be beaten and mangled by inordinate desires. They disbelieve divine judgments and evade human judgments, thinking that fortune will defend them from those who accuse them. They depict this "fortune" as blind, implying either that they are better than fortune, by which they think they are ruled, or that they themselves suffer from the same blindness. It is perfectly reasonable to admit that such people do everything by chance, since in whatever they do, they fall.[1] But we said enough in Book Two to combat this opinion, which is full of the most foolish and insane error.

Others, however, are not impertinent enough to deny that the providence of God rules over human life; but they prefer the

1. The Latin word for 'chance' ('*casus*') is derived from the verb 'to fall' ('*cado*').

wicked error of believing that it is weak, or unjust, or evil, rather than confessing their sins with humble supplication. If only they would let themselves be convinced that, when they think of what is best and most just and most powerful, the goodness and justice and power of God are far greater and far higher than anything they can conceive; if only they would consider themselves and understand that they would owe thanks to God even if he had willed to make them lower than they are. Then the very bone and marrow of their conscience would cry out, "I said, 'O Lord, have mercy upon me; heal my soul, for I have sinned against you'."[2] Thus they would be led in the secure paths of divine mercy along the road to wisdom, not becoming conceited when they made new discoveries or disheartened when they failed to do so. Their new knowledge would simply prepare them to see more, and their ignorance would make them more patient in seeking the truth. Of course I'm sure that you already believe this. But you will see how easily I can answer your difficult question once I have answered a few preliminary questions.

3.   Surely this is the problem that is disturbing and puzzling you. How is it that these two propositions are not contradictory and inconsistent: (1) God has foreknowledge of everything in the future; and (2) We sin by the will, not by necessity? For, you say, if God foreknows that someone is going to sin, then it is necessary that he sin. But if it is necessary, the will has no choice about whether to sin; there is an inescapable and fixed necessity. And so you fear that this argument forces us into one of two positions: either we draw the heretical conclusion that God does not foreknow everything in the future; or, if we cannot accept this conclusion, we must admit that sin happens by necessity and not by will. Isn't that what is bothering you?

EVODIUS: That's it exactly.

AUGUSTINE: So you think that anything that God foreknows happens by necessity and not by will.

EVODIUS: Precisely.

AUGUSTINE: Now pay close attention. Look inside yourself for a little while, and tell me, if you can, what sort of will you are going to have tomorrow: a will to do right or a will to sin?

---

2. Psalm 41:4

EVODIUS: I don't know.

AUGUSTINE: Do you think that God doesn't know either?

EVODIUS: Not at all—God certainly does know.

AUGUSTINE: Well then, if God knows what you are going to will tomorrow, and foresees the future wills of every human being, both those who exist now and those who will exist in the future, he surely foresees how he is going to treat the just and the irreligious.

EVODIUS: Clearly, if I say that God foreknows all of my actions, I can much more confidently say that he foreknows his own actions and foresees with absolute certainty what he is going to do.

AUGUSTINE: Then aren't you worried that someone might object that God himself will act out of necessity rather than by his will in everything that he is going to do? After all, you said that whatever God foreknows happens by necessity, not by will.

EVODIUS: When I said that, I was thinking only of what happens in his creation and not of what happens within himself. For those things do not come into being; they are eternal.

AUGUSTINE: So God does nothing in his creation.

EVODIUS: He has already established, once for all, the ways in which the universe that he created is to be governed; he does not administer anything by a new act of will.

AUGUSTINE: Doesn't he make anyone happy?

EVODIUS: Of course he does.

AUGUSTINE: And he does this when that person is made happy.

EVODIUS: Right.

AUGUSTINE: Then suppose, for example, that you are going to be happy a year from now. That means that a year from now God is going to make you happy.

EVODIUS: That's right too.

AUGUSTINE: And God knows today what he is going to do a year from now.

EVODIUS: He has always foreknown this, so I admit that he foreknows it now, if indeed it is really going to happen.

AUGUSTINE: Then surely you are not God's creature, or else your happiness does not take place in you.

EVODIUS: But I am God's creature, and my happiness does take place in me.

AUGUSTINE: Then the happiness that God gives you takes place by necessity and not by will.

Evodius: His will *is* my necessity.

Augustine: And so you will be happy against your will.

Evodius: If I had the power to be happy I would be happy right now. Even now I will to be happy, but I'm not, since it is God who makes me happy. I cannot do it for myself.

Augustine: How clearly the truth speaks through you! You could not help thinking that the only thing that is within our power is that which we do when we will it. Therefore, nothing is so much within our power as the will itself, for it is near at hand the very moment that we will. So we can rightly say, "We grow old by necessity, not by will"; or "We become feeble by necessity, not by will"; or "We die by necessity, not by will," and other such things. But who would be crazy enough to say "We do not will by the will"? Therefore, although God foreknows what we are going to will in the future, it does not follow that we do not will by the will.

When you said that you cannot make yourself happy, you said it as if I had denied it. Not at all; I am merely saying that when you do become happy, it will be in accordance with your will, not against your will. Simply because God foreknows your future happiness—and nothing can happen except as God foreknows it, since otherwise it would not be foreknowledge—it does not follow that you will be happy against your will. That would be completely absurd and far from the truth. So God's foreknowledge, which is certain even today of your future happiness, does not take away your will for happiness once you have begun to be happy; and in the same way, your blameworthy will (if indeed you are going to have such a will) does not cease to be a will simply because God foreknows that you are going to have it.

Just notice how imperceptive someone would have to be to argue thus: "If God has foreknown my future will, it is necessary that I will what he has foreknown, since nothing can happen otherwise than as he has foreknown it. But if it is necessary, then one must concede that I will it by necessity and not by will." What extraordinary foolishness! If God foreknew a future will that turned out not to be a will at all, things would indeed happen otherwise than as God foreknew them. And I will overlook this objector's equally monstrous statement that "it is necessary that I will," for by assuming necessity he tries to abolish will. For if his willing is necessary, how does he will, since there is no will?

Suppose he expressed it in another way and said that, since his willing is necessary, his will is not in his own power. This would run up against the same problem that you had when I asked whether you were going to be happy against your will. You replied that you would already be happy if you had the power; you said that you have the will but not the power. I answered that the truth had spoken through you. For we can deny that something is in our power only if it is not present even when we will it; but if we will, and yet the will remains absent, then we are not really willing at all. Now if it is impossible for us not to will when we are willing, then the will is present to those who will; and if something is present when we will it, then it is in our power. So our will would not be a will if it were not in our power. And since it is in our power, we are free with respect to it. But we are not free with respect to anything that we do not have in our power, and anything that we have cannot be nothing.

Thus, we believe both that God has foreknowledge of everything in the future and that nonetheless we will whatever we will. Since God foreknows our will, the very will that he foreknows will be what comes about. Therefore, it will be a will, since it is a will that he foreknows. And it could not be a will unless it were in our power. Therefore, he also foreknows this power. It follows, then, that his foreknowledge does not take away my power; in fact, it is all the more certain that I will have that power, since he whose foreknowledge never errs foreknows that I will have it.

EVODIUS: I agree now that it is necessary that whatever God has foreknown will happen, and that he foreknows our sins in such a way that our wills remain free and are within our power.

AUGUSTINE: Then what is troubling you? Have you perhaps for- **4.** gotten the results of our first discussion? Will you deny that nothing at all, whether superior, equal, or inferior, can coerce the will, and that we sin by our own wills?

EVODIUS: I certainly wouldn't dream of denying any of those things. But still, I must admit that I can't quite see how God's foreknowledge of our sins can be consistent with our free choice in sinning. For we must admit that God is just, and that he has foreknowledge. But I would like to know how it can be just to punish sins that happen necessarily, or how things that God foreknows do not happen necessarily, or how whatever happens necessarily in creation should not be attributed to the Creator.

AUGUSTINE: Why do you think that our free choice is inconsistent with God's foreknowledge? Because it's foreknowledge, or because it's *God's* foreknowledge?

EVODIUS: Because it's God's foreknowledge.

AUGUSTINE: If you knew that someone was going to sin, he wouldn't sin necessarily, would he?

EVODIUS: Indeed he would. Unless I foreknew something with certainty, it wouldn't be foreknowledge at all.

AUGUSTINE: Then it's not *God's* foreknowledge that makes his sin necessary, but any foreknowledge, since if something is not foreknown with certainty, it is not foreknown at all.

EVODIUS: I agree. But where are you headed with this?

AUGUSTINE: Unless I am mistaken, you do not force someone to sin just because you foreknow that he is going to sin. Nor does your foreknowledge force him to sin, even if he is undoubtedly going to sin—since otherwise you would not have genuine foreknowledge. So if your foreknowledge is consistent with his freedom in sinning, so that you foreknow what someone else is going to do by his own will, then God forces no one to sin, even though he foresees those who are going to sin by their own will.

Why then can't our just God punish those things that his foreknowledge does not force to happen? Just as your memory does not force the past to have happened, God's foreknowledge does not force the future to happen. And just as you remember some things that you have done but did not do everything that you remember, God foreknows everything that he causes but does not cause everything that he foreknows. Of such things he is not the evil cause, but the just avenger. Therefore, you must understand that God justly punishes the sins that he foreknows but does not cause. If the fact that God foresees their sins means that he should not punish sinners, then he should also not reward those who act rightly, for he also foresees their righteous actions. Let us rather confess that nothing in the future is hidden from God's foreknowledge, and that no sin is left unpunished by his justice, for sin is committed by the will, not coerced by God's foreknowledge.

5.   As for your third question, about how the Creator can escape blame for whatever happens necessarily in his creation, it will

not easily overcome that rule of piety that we ought to bear in mind, namely, that we owe thanks to our Creator. His most abundant goodness would be most justly praised even if he had created us at a lower level of creation. For even though our souls are decayed with sin, they are better and more sublime than they would be if they were transformed into visible light. And you see that even souls that are addicted to the bodily senses give God great praise for the grandeur of light. Therefore, don't let the fact that sinful souls are condemned lead you to say in your heart that it would be better if they did not exist. For they are condemned only in comparison with what they would have been if they had refused to sin. Nonetheless, God their Creator deserves the most noble praise that human beings can offer him, not only because he places them in a just order when they sin, but also because he created them in such a way that even the filth of sin could in no way make them inferior to corporeal light, for which he is nonetheless praised.

So you should not say that it would be better if sinful souls had never existed. But I must also warn you not to say that they ought to have been created differently. Whatever might rightly occur to you as being better, you may be sure that God, as the Creator of all good things, has made that too. When you think that something better should have been made, it is not right reason, but grudging weakness, to will that nothing lower had been made, as if you looked upon the heavens and wished that the earth had not been made. Such a wish is utterly unjust.

If you saw that the earth had been made but not the heavens, then you would have a legitimate complaint, for you could say that the earth ought to have been made like the heavens that you can imagine. But since you see that the pattern to which you wanted the earth to conform has indeed been made (but it is called 'the heavens' and not 'the earth'), I'm sure that you would not begrudge the fact that the inferior thing has also been made, and that the earth exists, since you are not deprived of the better thing. And there is so great a variety of parts in the earth that we cannot conceive of any earthly form that God has not created. By intermediate steps one passes gradually from the most fertile and pleasant land to the briniest and most barren, so that you would not dream of disparaging any of them except in comparison with a better. Thus you ascend through every degree of praise, so that even when you come to the very best land, you would not want it to exist without the others. And how great a distance there is between the whole earth and the heavens! For between the two is interposed the watery and airy nature. From these four elements come a variety of forms and species too numerous for us to count, although God has numbered them all.

Therefore, it is possible for something to exist in the universe that you do not conceive with your reason, but it is not possible for something that you conceive by right reason not to exist. For you cannot conceive anything better in creation that has slipped the mind of the Creator. Indeed, the human soul is naturally connected with the divine reasons on which it depends. When it says "It would be better to make this than that," if what it says is true, and it sees what it is saying, then it sees that truth in the reasons to which it is connected. If, therefore, it knows by right reason that God ought to have made something, let it believe that God has in fact done so, even if it does not see the thing among those that God has made.

For example, suppose we could not see the heavens. Nonetheless, if right reason showed that some such thing ought to have been made, it would be right for us to believe that it was made, even if we did not see it with our own eyes. For if we see by thought that something ought to have been made, we see it only in those reasons by which all things were made. But no truthful thinking can enable someone to see what is not in those reasons, for whatever is not there is not true.

Many people go astray when they have seen better things with their mind because in searching for it with their eyes they look in the wrong places. They are like someone who understands perfect roundness and is angry because he does not find it in a nut, if that is the only round object that he sees. In the same way, some people see by the truest reason that a creature is better if it is so firmly dedicated to God that it will never sin, even though it has free will. Then, when they look upon the sins of human beings, they do not use their sorrow over sin to stop people from sinning; they bemoan the fact that human beings were created in the first place. "He ought to have made us," they say, "so that we would always enjoy his unchangeable truth, so that we would never will to sin." Let them not moan and complain! God, who gave them the power to will, did not force them to sin; and there are angels who never have sinned and never will sin.

Therefore, if you take delight in a creature whose will is so perfectly steadfast that he does not sin, it is by right reason that you prefer this creature to one that sins. And just as you give it a higher rank in your thinking, the Creator gave it a higher rank in his ordering. So be sure that such a creature exists in the higher places and in the splendor of the heavens, since if the Creator manifested his goodness in creating something that he foresaw would sin, he certainly manifested his goodness in creating something that he foreknew would not sin.

That sublime creature has perpetual happiness in the perpetual enjoyment of its Creator, a happiness that it deserves because it perpetually wills to retain justice. Next, there is a proper place even for the sinful nature that by its sins has lost happiness but not thrown away the power to recover happiness. This nature is in turn higher than one that perpetually wills to sin. It occupies a sort of intermediate position between those that persist in willing justice and those that persist in willing to sin. It receives its greatness from the lowliness of repentance.

But God, in the bounty of his goodness, did not shrink from creating even that creature whom he foreknew would not merely sin, but would persist in willing to sin. For a runaway horse is better than a stone that stays in the right place only because it has no movement or perception of its own; and in the same way, a creature that sins by free will is more excellent than one that does not sin only because it has no free will. I would praise wine as a thing good of its kind, but condemn a person who got drunk on that wine. And yet I would prefer that person, condemned and drunk, to the wine that I praised, on which he got drunk. In the same way, the material creation is rightly praised on its own level, but those who turn away from the perception of the truth by immoderately using the material creation deserve condemnation. And yet even those perverse and drunken people who are ruined by this greed are to be preferred to the material creation, praiseworthy though it is in its own order, not because of the merit of their sins, but because of the dignity of their nature.

Therefore, any soul is better than any material object. Now no sinful soul, however far it may fall, is ever changed into a material

object; it never ceases to be a soul. Therefore, no soul ceases to
be better than a material object. Consequently, the lowest soul is
still better than light, which is the foremost among material
objects. It may be that the body in which a certain soul exists is
inferior to some other body, but the soul itself can in no way be
inferior to a body.

Why, then, should we not praise God with unspeakable praise,
simply because when he made those souls who would persevere
in the laws of justice, he made others who he foresaw would sin,
even some who would persevere in sin? For even such souls are
better than souls that cannot sin because they lack reason and
the free choice of the will. And these souls are in turn better than
the brilliance of any material object, however splendid, which
some people mistakenly worship instead of the Most High God.
In the order of material creation, from the heavenly choirs to the
number of the hairs of our heads, the beauty of good things at
every level is so perfectly harmonious that only the most ignorant
could say, "What is this? Why is this?"—for all things were created
in their proper order. How much more ignorant, then, to say this
of a soul whose glory, however dimmed and tarnished it might
become, far exceeds the dignity of any material object!

Reason judges in one way, custom in another. Reason judges
by the light of truth, so that by right judgment it subjects lesser
things to greater. Custom is often swayed by agreeable habits, so
that it esteems as greater what truth reveals as lower. Reason
accords the heavenly bodies far greater honor than earthly bodies.
And yet who among carnal human beings would not much rather
have many stars gone from the heavens than one sapling missing
from his field or one cow from his pasture? Children would rather
see a man die (unless it is someone they love) than their pet bird,
especially if the man frightens them and the bird is beautiful and
can sing; but adults utterly despise their judgments, or at least
wait patiently until they can be corrected. In the same way, there
are those who praise God for his lesser creatures, which are better
suited to their carnal senses. But when it comes to his superior
and better creatures, some of these people praise him less or not
at all; some even try to find fault with them or change them; and
some do not believe that God created them. But those who have
advanced along the road to wisdom regard such people as ignorant judges of things. Until they can correct the ignorant, they

learn to bear with them patiently; but if they cannot correct them, they utterly repudiate their judgments.

Since this is the case, it is quite wrong to think that the sins of **6.** the creature should be attributed to the Creator, even though it is necessary that whatever he foreknows will happen. So much so, that when you said you could find no way to avoid attributing to him everything in his creation that happens necessarily, I on the other hand could find no way—nor can any way be found, for I am convinced that there is no way—to attribute to him anything in his creation that happens necessarily by the will of sinners.

Someone might say, "I would rather not exist at all than be unhappy." I would reply, "You're lying. You're unhappy now, and the only reason you don't want to die is to go on existing. You don't want to be unhappy, but you do want to exist. Give thanks, therefore, for what you are willingly, so that what you are against your will might be taken away; for you willingly exist, but you are unhappy against your will. If you are ungrateful for what you will to be, you are justly compelled to be what you do not will. So I praise the goodness of your Creator, for even though you are ungrateful you have what you will; and I praise the justice of your Lawgiver, for because you are ungrateful you suffer what you do not will."

But then he might say, "It is not because I would rather be unhappy than not exist at all that I am unwilling to die; it's because I'm afraid that I might be even more unhappy after death." I would reply, "If it is unjust for you to be even more unhappy, you won't be so; but if it is just, let us praise him by whose laws you will be so."

Next he might ask, "Why should I assume that if it is unjust I won't be more unhappy?" I would reply, "If at that time you are in your own power, either you will not be unhappy, or you will be governing yourself unjustly, in which case you will deserve your unhappiness. But suppose instead that you wish to govern yourself justly but cannot. That means that you are not in your own power, so either someone else has power over you, or no one has. If no one has power over you, you will act either willingly or unwillingly. It cannot be unwillingly, because nothing happens to you unwillingly unless you are overcome by some force, and you cannot be overcome by any force if no one has power over you. And if it is willingly, you are in fact in your own power, and the earlier argument applies: either you deserve your unhappiness for governing yourself unjustly, or, since you have whatever you will, you have reason to give thanks for the goodness of your Creator.

"Therefore, if you are not in your own power, some other thing must have control over you. This thing is either stronger or weaker than you. If it is weaker than you, your servitude is your own fault and your unhappiness is just, since you could overpower this thing if you willed to do so. And if a stronger thing has control over you, its control is in accordance with proper order, and you cannot rightly think that so right an order is unjust. I was therefore quite correct to say, 'If it is unjust for you to be even more unhappy, you won't be so; but if it is just, let us praise him by whose laws you will be so'."

7.   Then he might say, "The only reason that I will to be unhappy rather than not to exist at all is that I already exist; if somehow I could have been consulted on this matter before I existed, I would have chosen not to exist rather than to be unhappy. The fact that I am now afraid not to exist, even though I am unhappy, is itself part of that very unhappiness because of which I do not will what I ought to will. For I ought to will not to exist rather than to be unhappy. And yet I admit that in fact I would rather be unhappy than be nothing. But the more unhappy I am, the more foolish I am to will this; and the more truly I see that I ought not will this, the more unhappy I am."

I would reply, "Be careful that you are not mistaken when you think you see the truth. For if you were happy, you would certainly prefer existence to nonexistence. Even as it is, although you are unhappy and do not will to be unhappy, you would rather exist and be unhappy than not exist at all. Consider, then, as well as you can, how great is the good of existence, which the happy and the unhappy alike will. If you consider it well, you will realize three things. First, you are unhappy to the extent that you are far from him who exists in the highest degree. Second, the more you think that it is better for someone not to exist than to be unhappy, the less you will see him who exists in the highest degree. Finally, you nonetheless will to exist because you are from him who exists in the highest degree."

So if you will to escape from unhappiness, cherish your will to exist. For if you will more and more to exist, you will approach him who exists in the highest degree. And give thanks that you exist now, for even though you are inferior to those who are happy, you are superior to things that do not have even the will to be happy—and many such things are praised even by those who are unhappy. Nonetheless, all things that exist deserve praise simply in virtue of the fact that they exist, for they are good simply in virtue of the fact that they exist.

The more you love existence, the more you will desire eternal life, and so the more you will long to be refashioned so that your affections are no longer temporal, branded upon you by the love of temporal things that are nothing before they exist, and then, once they do exist, flee from existence until they exist no more. And so when their existence is still to come, they do not yet exist; and when their existence is past, they exist no more. How can you expect such things to endure, when for them to begin to exist is to set out on the road to nonexistence?

Someone who loves existence approves of such things insofar as they exist and loves that which always exists. If once he used to waver in the love of temporal things, he now grows firm in the love of the eternal. Once he wallowed in the love of fleeting things, but he will stand steadfast in the love of what is permanent. Then he will obtain the very existence that he willed when he was afraid not to exist but could not stand upright because he was entangled in the love of fleeting things.

Therefore, do not grieve that you would rather exist and be unhappy than not exist and be nothing at all. Instead, rejoice greatly, for your will to exist is like a first step. If you go on from there to set your sights more and more on existence, you will rise to him who exists in the highest degree. Thus you will keep yourself from the kind of fall in which that which exists in the lowest degree ceases to exist and thereby devastates the one who loves it. Hence, someone who prefers not to exist rather than to be unhappy has no choice but to be unhappy, since he cannot fail to exist; but someone who loves existence more than he hates being unhappy can banish what he hates by cleaving more and more to what he loves. For someone who has come to enjoy an existence that is perfect for a thing of his kind cannot be unhappy.

Notice how absurd and illogical it would be to say "I would **8.** prefer not to exist rather than to be unhappy." For someone who says "I would prefer this rather than that" is choosing something. But not to exist is not something, but nothing. Therefore, you can't properly choose it, since what you are choosing does not exist.

Perhaps you will say that you do in fact will to exist, even though you are unhappy, but that you *shouldn't* will to exist. Then what should you will? "Not to exist," you say. Well, if that is what you ought to will, it must be better; but that which does not exist cannot be better. Therefore, you should not will not to exist, and the frame of mind that keeps you from willing it is closer to the truth than your belief that you ought to will it.

Furthermore, if someone is right in choosing to pursue something, it must be the case that he becomes better when he attains it. But whoever does not exist cannot be better, and so no one can be right in choosing not to exist. We should not be swayed by the judgment of those whose unhappiness has driven them to suicide. Either they thought that they would be better off after death, in which case they were doing nothing contrary to our argument (whether they were right in thinking so or not); or else they thought that they would be nothing after death, in which case there is even less reason for us to bother with them, since they falsely chose nothing. For how am I supposed to concur in the choice of someone who, if I asked him what he was choosing, would say "Nothing"? And someone who chooses not to exist is clearly choosing nothing, even if he won't admit it.

To tell you quite frankly what I think about this whole issue, it seems to me that someone who kills himself or in some way wants to die has the feeling that he will not exist after death, whatever his conscious opinion may be. Opinion, whether true or false, has to do with reason or faith; but feeling derives its power from either habit or nature. It can happen that opinion leads in one direction and feeling in another. This is easy to see in cases where we believe that we ought to do one thing but enjoy doing just the opposite. And sometimes feeling is closer to the truth than opinion is, as when the opinion is in error and the feeling is from nature. For example, a sick man will often enjoy drinking cold water, which is good for him, even if he believes that it will kill him. But sometimes opinion is closer to the truth than feeling is, as when someone's knowledge of medicine tells him that cold water would be harmful when in fact it *would* be harmful, even though it would be pleasant to drink. Sometimes both are right, as when one rightly believes that something is beneficial and also finds it pleasing. Sometimes both are wrong, as when one believes that something is beneficial when it is actually harmful and one is also happy not to give it up.

It often happens that right opinion corrects perverted habits and that perverted opinion distorts an upright nature, so great is the power of the dominion and rule of reason. Therefore, someone who believes that after death he will not exist is driven by his unbearable troubles to desire death with all his heart; he chooses death and takes hold of it. His opinion is completely false, but his feeling is simply a natural desire for peace. And something that has peace is not nothing; indeed, it is greater than something that is restless. For restlessness generates one conflicting passion after another, whereas peace has the constancy that is the most conspicuous characteristic of Being.

So the will's desire for death is not a desire for nonexistence but a desire for peace. When someone wrongly believes that he will not exist, he desires by nature to be at peace; that is, he desires to exist in a higher degree. Therefore, just as no one can desire not to exist, no one ought to be ungrateful to the goodness of the Creator for the fact that he exists.

Perhaps someone might say, "It would not have been terribly **9.** difficult or troublesome for an omnipotent God to place all his creatures in such an order that none of them would ever be unhappy. For if he is omnipotent, he could not have lacked the power to do so; and if he is good, he would not have begrudged his creatures such happiness."

I would reply that the order of creation proceeds from the highest to the lowest by just degrees. It is pure spite to say that something in that creation ought to be different, or shouldn't exist at all. It is wrong to want one thing to be like something else that is superior to it, for the superior thing already exists in such a way that it would be wrong to add to it, since it is perfect. Therefore, someone who says "This thing ought to be like that one" either wants to add to the perfect and superior creature, and so he is immoderate and unjust; or else he wants to destroy the lower creature, and so he is wicked and spiteful.

But someone who says "This thing ought not to exist" is no less wicked and spiteful, since the thing that he wants not to exist, although inferior, clearly deserves praise. For example, someone might say, "The moon ought not to exist," all the while admitting (or foolishly and contentiously denying) that even the light of a lamp, which is vastly inferior, is beautiful in its own class; it adorns earthly darkness and is useful at night; and for all of these reasons it deserves praise in its own small way. How then can he properly say that the moon should not exist, when he would laugh at himself for saying that lamps should not exist? But perhaps, instead of saying that the moon should not exist at all, he would say that the moon ought to be as he sees the sun to be. This amounts to saying, "The moon should not exist, but there should be two suns." In this way he makes two mistakes: by desiring another sun, he tries to add to the perfection of creation; and by wanting to take away the moon, he tries to weaken that perfection.

Perhaps he would say that he has no complaint about the moon, since its inferior brightness does not make it unhappy; his complaint is about souls. And it is not their darkness that grieves him; it is their unhappiness. He should think very carefully about the fact that the brightness of the moon is not unhappy and the brightness of the sun is not happy. For although they are celestial bodies, they are still material objects, at least insofar as they pertain to the light that we can perceive with our physical eyes. And material objects as such cannot be happy or unhappy, although they can serve as the bodies of those who are happy or unhappy.

But our analogy about the sun and moon shows us one thing. When you observe the differences among material objects and see that some are brighter than others, it would be wrong to want to get rid of the darker ones, or to make them just like the brighter ones. Instead, if you refer all of them to the perfection of the whole, you will see that these differences in brightness contribute to the more perfect being of the universe. The universe would not be perfect unless the greater things were present in such a way that lesser things are not excluded. In the same way, when you consider the differences among souls, you will find that the unhappiness that grieves you also contributes to the perfection of the whole by ensuring that it includes even those souls who deserved to be made unhappy because they willed to be sinners. God was perfectly justified in making such souls, just as he deserves praise for making other creatures that are far inferior even to unhappy souls.

Someone who did not quite understand what I have said might raise this objection: "If our unhappiness completes the perfection of the whole, then this perfection would be missing something if we were always happy. Therefore, if no soul becomes unhappy except by sinning, it follows that even our sins are necessary to the perfection of the universe that God created. How then can God justly punish our sins when they are necessary to ensure that his creation is complete and perfect?"

The answer is this. What is necessary to the perfection of the universe is not our sins or our unhappiness, but the existence of souls that, simply because they are souls, sin if they so will and become unhappy if they sin. If unhappiness preceded our sins or continued after those sins were taken away, you would be right to say that the order and administration of the universe was defective. But it would be no less a blot on this order if sins existed but not unhappiness. When those who do not sin are happy, the universe is perfect; but when those who sin are unhappy, the universe is no less perfect. The fact that there are souls that will be unhappy if they sin and happy if they do not sin means that the universe is complete and perfect with respect to every nature that it contains. Sin and the punishment for sin are not natures, but characteristics of natures, the former voluntary and the latter punitive. The voluntary characteristic that comes about when one sins is disgraceful, so the punitive characteristic is used to place the soul in an order where it is not disgraceful for such a soul to be, forcing it to conform to the beauty of the universe as a whole, so that the ugliness of sin is remedied by the punishment of sin.

Hence it happens that when a superior creature sins, it may be punished by inferior creatures, which are so humble that they can receive adornment even from souls in disgrace and thus conform to the beauty of the universe as a whole. For what is greater in a household than a human being? And what is lower and more contemptible than the sewer? And yet a servant who is punished for some great sin by being made to clean out the sewer lends dignity to the sewer even by his own disgrace. Both the disgrace of the servant and the cleaning of the sewer, when they are joined in this way and brought into a sort of unity, are woven together to serve the most orderly beauty of the household as a whole. Nonetheless, if the servant had not willed to sin, some other provision would have been made for cleaning the sewer.

And what is humbler in all creation than earthly bodies? Yet even a sinful soul lends dignity to this corruptible flesh by providing it with vital motion and a most beautiful form. Because of its sin, such a soul is not suited for a heavenly dwelling-place; but through its punishment it becomes suitable for an earthly dwelling-place. In this way, no matter what the soul chooses, every part of the universe is perfectly ordered into a beautiful whole, of which God is the creator and overseer. For the best souls lend dignity to the humblest creatures among whom they dwell, not by their unhappiness (for they are not unhappy), but by making good use of those creatures. But it would be unjust if sinful souls were permitted to dwell in the highest places, where they do not belong, since they cannot use superior creatures well or adorn them in any way.

Although this earthly globe is numbered among corruptible things, it preserves as much as possible the image of higher things, never ceasing to show them to us as examples and evidence. If we see a good and great man burned by fire (as far as his body is concerned) in the performance of his duty, we do not call this a punishment for sin, but a proof of his fortitude and patience, and we love him even more when his body has suffered the most revolting corruption than if he had not undergone anything like that. Indeed, we marvel that the nature of the soul is not changed by the mutability of the body. But when we see the body of a cruel robber afflicted with the same suffering, we approve the order of the laws. Both of these torments add beauty to the order of things, one by the merit of virtue and the other by the merit of sinfulness.

If after these fires, or even before them, we saw that most excellent man carried up into the heavens to a suitable dwelling-place, we would be glad indeed. But who could fail to be offended if we saw that criminal lifted up to heaven, whether before or after his punishment, and raised to a place of everlasting honor while still clinging to his evil will? Thus it is that both men can adorn inferior creatures, but only one of them can adorn superior creatures. By this we are reminded that the first human being adorned the mortality of this body so that his sin might find a fitting penalty, and our Lord adorned it so that his mercy might set us free from sin.

A just man who perseveres in justice might still have a mortal body, but a wicked man, as long as he remains wicked, cannot attain the immortality of the saints, an immortality that is sublime and angelic: not indeed like those angels of whom St. Paul says, "Do you not know that we are going to judge the angels?"[3] but like those of whom the Lord says, "They will be equal to the angels of God."[4] For those who desire equality with the angels for the sake of their own foolish self-aggrandizement do not really want to be equal to the angels; they want the angels to be equal to them. If they persevere in that will, they will receive equal punishment with the fallen angels, who loved their own power more than the omnipotence of God. And to those whom he has placed at his left hand because they led proud and unmerciful lives and did not seek God through the door of humility, which the Lord Jesus Christ shows in himself, he will say, "Depart into the eternal fire that has been prepared for the devil and his angels."[5]

There are two sources of sin: one's own spontaneous thought, **10.** and someone else's persuasion. I believe that the Psalmist was speaking of these when he wrote, "Cleanse me, O Lord, from my hidden faults, and spare your servant from those of others."[6] Now both of these are voluntary; just as no one sins unwillingly by his own thought, so no one yields to the evil prompting of another unless his own will consents. But it is more serious when one not only sins by one's own thought, with no prompting from anyone else, but also uses malice and guile to persuade someone else to sin, than it is to be brought to sin by someone else's persuasion. Therefore, God's justice is preserved when he punishes either sort of sin. The scales of justice have determined that human beings should not be free even from the power of the devil himself, to whom they capitulated when they listened to his evil persua-

---

3. 1 Corinthians 6:3

4. Cf. Matthew 22:30; Luke 20:36

5. Matthew 25:41. See the whole parable of the sheep and the goats, Matthew 25:31–46, especially verses 32–33 and 41–46.

6. Psalm 19:13

sion. For it would have been wrong if they were not ruled by the one who had taken them captive.

And yet the perfect justice of the True and Most High God, which is without limit, could not fail to bring order even to the downfall of sinners. Because human beings sinned less than the devil, their salvation was made easier by the very fact that they were given over until death to the prince of this world, of this mortal and base part of the universe, the prince of all sins and the ruler of death. For the consciousness of their mortality makes them timid. They grow to fear death or harm from the lowest, humblest, and smallest beasts. Uncertain of the future, they cling to illicit pleasures, and especially to the very pride that made them fall. Thus they grow weak, since that one vice of pride makes them spit out the medicine of mercy that would restore them. For who needs mercy more than one who is wretched? And who is more unworthy of mercy than one who is wretched and proud?

For this reason it came to pass that the Word of God, through whom all things were made and whom all the happy angels enjoy, stretched forth his mercy even to our wretchedness; he became flesh and dwelt among us. Thus even before human beings were made equal to the angels, they were able to eat the bread of angels, for that bread had deigned to become equal to human beings. But he did not abandon them when he came down to us; he remained wholly present with them even as he was wholly present with us. Through his divine nature he nourishes them from within, but through our human nature he admonishes us from without. By faith he makes us fit to feed like the angels on the light of his presence. For the Word is the best food of the rational creature, and the human soul is indeed rational, even though in punishment for its sin it was bound by the chains of mortality and brought so low that it must try to understand invisible things by conjectures drawn from visible things. That food of the rational creature became visible—not by changing his own nature but by putting on ours—so that he might recall the followers of visible things to himself, the invisible Word. Thus the soul that forsook him out of its inward pride, finding him in outward humility, will imitate his visible humility and return with him to his invisible greatness.

Thus the Word of God, the only Son of God, put on our human nature and brought the devil, who always was and always will be subject to his laws, under subjection to that human nature. He did not wrest control from the devil by violence, but overcame him by the law of justice. For ever since the devil deceived the woman and through her the man, he laid claim to all the offspring of the human race and made them subject to his laws of death, because they were sinners. He did this out of a malicious desire to do harm, but it was sanctioned by a most equitable law.

But he upheld this claim only so long as his power endured, that is, until he killed that just man in whom he could show nothing worthy of death. For not only was he killed without any crime, he was also born without the inordinate desire to which the devil had enslaved those whom he had taken prisoner, so that whatever was born out of inordinate desire would be his, like the fruit of his own tree. Although his desire to hold on to this fruit was depraved, the law by which he possessed it was just. And so he is most justly compelled to release those who believe in the one whom he unjustly killed. Thus, when they die temporally, they pay their debt; and when they live eternally, they live in him who on their behalf paid what he did not owe. But those whom the devil persuades to persevere in unbelief are justly given to him as his companions in eternal damnation.

Thus it was not by force that human beings were rescued from the devil, who had captured them by persuasion and not by force. As they were justly humbled to serve the devil, to whom they gave consent for evil, so they were justly set free by Christ, to whom they gave consent for good. For they sinned less by giving their consent than the devil sinned by his evil persuasion.

So God made every nature, not only those who would persevere **11.** in virtue and justice, but also those who would sin. But he did not make them so that they would sin; he made them to adorn the universe, whether or not they willed to sin. There are some souls that hold such preeminence in the order of creation that their will to sin would weaken and destroy the universe. If they had not existed, creation would have been missing a great good, for it would have lacked the very thing whose absence throws the stability and interconnection of created things into chaos. Such are the best creatures, the holy and sublime creatures of the celestial and super-celestial powers, whom God alone commands, but to whom the whole world is subject. Without their just and perfect activity the universe could not exist.

There are other souls who would not weaken the order of the universe whether they sinned or not, and yet here again creation would have been missing a great good if they had not existed. These are rational souls, who are inferior in activity but equal in nature to those superior souls. And the Most High God created many levels of things that are inferior even to rational souls, but even these things deserve praise.

The natures that exercise a more sublime activity are such that the order of the universe would be weakened if they did not exist, or even if they sinned. The natures that exercise an inferior activity are such that the universe would be missing something if they did not exist, but not if they sinned. The higher natures were given complete power to maintain their proper activity, which could not be missing from the order of things. They did not persevere in their good will because they received this activity; rather, they received this activity because God, who gave it to them, foresaw that they would persevere. They do not control all things by their own majesty, but by cleaving to the divine majesty and most devotedly obeying the commands of God, from whom and through whom and in whom all things were made.

The lower natures too were given the power to control all things, so long as they did not sin. But this activity was not to be theirs alone; they were to share it with those higher natures, because God foreknew that the lower natures would sin. Spiritual natures come together without aggregation and separate without diminution, so that the activity of the higher is not made easier by the help of the lower or more difficult when the lower abandons its activity by sinning. For two spiritual natures can be joined by similarity of disposition and separated by dissimilarity, but not by place or physical bulk, even if each of them has a body.

The nature that was ordained to dwell among inferior and mortal bodies governs a body of its own. But after it has sinned, it no longer rules its body exactly as it chooses, but only as the laws of the universe allow. This does not mean that such a soul is inferior to a celestial body, although earthly bodies are inferior to celestial bodies. The tattered clothing of a servant who has fallen out of favor is vastly inferior to the clothing of a well-deserving servant who is greatly honored by his master; but the servant himself is better than any fine clothing, since he is a human being. The higher nature cleaves to God, and in its celestial body, through its angelic power, it adorns and rules even terrestrial bodies in accordance with the decrees of God, whose will it beholds in an ineffable way. But the lower nature that is burdened with a mortal body can scarcely govern the body that drags it down; nonetheless, it adorns the body as well as it can. It also tries to affect the other things that are near it, but over them its power is even feebler.

It follows, therefore, that the humblest part of material creation **12.** would not have lacked a most suitable adornment, even if human beings had not willed to sin. Whatever can govern the whole can also govern the part, but something that is able to do lesser things is not necessarily able to do greater. A perfect doctor can also cure an itch, but not everyone who can profitably be consulted about an itch can restore the whole of human health. And if you see a clear reason why it was fitting that there be a creature that never sinned and never will sin, that same reason will also show that such a creature refrained from sinning by its own free will. It was not compelled not to sin; it refrained from sin voluntarily.

But even if it had sinned (although it didn't, just as God knew that it wouldn't), the unutterable might of the power of God would have sufficed to govern this universe. By granting to each creature a fitting and just reward, he would have allowed nothing base or unbecoming in all his dominions. If every angelic nature had deserted his precepts by sinning, God would have ruled all things in the best and most fitting way by his own majesty, without any of those angelic powers who were created to share in that rule. He would not have begrudged the immaterial creation its existence, for in the bounty of his goodness he established even the material creation, which is vastly inferior even to sinful spirits. No one who reasonably considers the heavens and the earth, and the measure, form, and order of all the visible natures in their kinds, can think that they have any creator other than God, or fail to confess that he is to be praised with unspeakable praise. But there is no better ordering of things than when the angelic power, by reason of the excellence of its nature and the goodness of its will, is preeminent in the administration of the universe.

Nonetheless, even if all the angels had sinned, they would not have left the Creator of the angels helpless to rule his own dominions. Out of his tireless goodness and effortless omnipotence, he would have created others, and stationed them at the posts that the first angels had deserted by sinning. Although they earned damnation, no spiritual creatures, however numerous, could destroy the order that has a fitting and becoming place for all the damned. So wherever we look, we find that God, the best Creator and most just Ruler of all natures, deserves unspeakable praise. Finally, let us leave the contemplation of the beauty of things to those to whom God has given the power to see it, and not try to use words to induce them to look upon things that cannot be expressed in speech. And yet, for the sake of the loquacious, the weak, and the contentious, let us explore this great question in the briefest possible way.

13.   Every nature that can become less good is good, and every nature becomes less good when it is corrupted. For either corruption does it no harm, in which case it is not being corrupted, or else it is indeed corrupted, in which case the corruption does in fact harm it. And if corruption harms it, it diminishes its goodness to some extent and thus makes it less good. If corruption leaves it bereft of any good at all, then whatever is left cannot be corrupted. For corruption can inflict no further harm, since there is no goodness left for it to take away. But if corruption cannot harm a nature, that nature cannot be corrupted; and if a nature cannot be corrupted, it is incorruptible. This leads to the absurd conclusion that a nature becomes incorruptible by undergoing corruption. Therefore, we must say that every nature is good insofar as it is a nature.

For every nature is either corruptible or incorruptible. If it is an incorruptible nature, it is better than a corruptible nature; and if it is a corruptible nature, it is undoubtedly good, since corruption makes it less good. Therefore, every nature is good. By 'nature' I mean what is also commonly called 'substance'.[7] So every sub-

---

7. The word 'substance' is used in philosophy principally to designate the individual thing that exists, as opposed to the characteristics ("accidents") that it has. For example, a cat is a substance; its color and size are accidents. 'Substance' can also mean a *kind* or *species* of thing. Augustine uses the word 'nature' in both these senses.

stance either is God or comes from God, since every good thing
either is God or comes from God.

Bearing these conclusions firmly in mind from the outset, pay
close attention to what I say. Every rational nature that was created with free choice of the will undoubtedly deserves praise if
it abides in the highest and unchangeable good; and every nature
that strives to abide there also deserves praise. But every nature
that does not abide there, and does not will to act so that it might
abide there, deserves to be condemned for precisely those reasons.

Therefore, if the created rational nature is praised, no one
doubts that its Creator deserves praise. And if it is condemned,
no one doubts that the Creator receives praise in that very condemnation. For we condemn it precisely because it does not will
to enjoy its Creator, who is the highest and unchangeable good;
but the Creator himself we do not hesitate to praise.

How good is God, the Creator of all things! Let every tongue
and every thought offer him unspeakable praise and honor! For
whether we ourselves are praised or condemned, God is always
praised. If we are condemned because we do not abide in him,
it is because our great and highest and foremost good is to abide
in him. And how can this be, unless he is a good beyond descrip-
tion? Then what can we find to condemn him for in our sins,
when we cannot condemn our sins without praising him?

If we condemn something, it is only because of some flaw that
it has. But we cannot condemn a flaw in something without
thereby praising the nature in which the flaw is present. For
there are two possibilities. On the one hand, perhaps what you
condemn is in accordance with the nature. In that case, it is no
flaw, and you need to learn how to appraise things properly, but
the thing you condemn needs no change at all. On the other hand,
perhaps it is indeed a flaw and you are right to condemn it. Then
the flaw must be contrary to the nature, for every flaw, insofar
as it is a flaw, is contrary to some nature. For if it does not harm
the nature, it is no flaw; but if it is a flaw precisely because it
harms the nature, then it is a flaw precisely because it is contrary
to the nature.

But it is unjust to condemn a nature that is corrupted, not by
its own flaw, but by a flaw in another nature. We must look
further to see whether the other nature in turn is corrupted by
its own flaw, a flaw by which that first nature is corrupted. For

what does it mean to ruin something, if not to corrupt it by some flaw? And a nature that is not being ruined lacks any flaw, whereas a nature whose flaw corrupts some other nature surely has a flaw. Such a nature is already flawed; it has already been corrupted by some flaw of its own, and only then can some other nature be corrupted by that flaw.

From this it follows that every flaw is contrary to some nature; more specifically, every flaw is contrary to the nature of the thing in which the flaw is present. Therefore, since nothing is condemned except a flaw, it is a flaw precisely because it is contrary to the nature of the thing in which it is present; and if a flaw is justly condemned, the nature in which it is present is thereby praised. For what justly displeases you in the flaw is that it spoils what pleases you in the nature.

14.   We must also see whether it is correct to say that a nature can be corrupted by a flaw in some other nature, without an associated flaw of its own. If a nature that attempts to use its own flaw to corrupt another nature does not find something corruptible in that other nature, it cannot corrupt it. If it does find something corruptible, however, it uses that flaw in the other nature to bring about its corruption. For a stronger thing cannot be corrupted by a weaker unless it wills to be corrupted; and if it wills to be corrupted, it has already begun to be corrupted through its own flaw and not through something else's.

And it is no less true that nothing can be corrupted by its equal unless it wills to be corrupted. If a flawed nature approaches a nature that has no flaw and attempts to corrupt it, it does not approach it as an equal; the flawed nature is weaker precisely because it is flawed. But if a stronger nature corrupts a weaker, either it happens through a flaw in both, if both act out of perverted desire; or else it happens through a flaw in the more powerful nature, if that nature is so much superior that it remains more powerful even when it has become flawed. For who can rightly condemn the fruits of the earth simply because human beings, corrupted by their own vice, do not use them well, but corrupt them by misusing them for their own illicit pleasure? Only a madman could doubt that human nature, even when it has become flawed, is more excellent and more powerful than any fruit, flawed or not.

It can also happen that a more powerful nature corrupts an

inferior nature, even though this happens through no flaw in either of them, if by a flaw we mean anything that deserves to be condemned. For who would presume to condemn a temperate person who seeks out the fruits of the earth only to maintain his life? And who would condemn those fruits themselves just because they are corrupted when they are used for food? Indeed, we do not generally call this 'corruption', since 'corruption' is ordinarily used to designate some flaw.

Furthermore, it is easy to find cases in which a stronger nature corrupts an inferior even without using it to satisfy some need. This comes about in one of two ways. First, a superior nature corrupts an inferior in the order of justice when it punishes it for some fault. As St. Paul put it, "If someone corrupts the temple of God, God will corrupt him."[8]

Second, a superior nature corrupts an inferior in the order of changeable things, which yield to one another in accordance with suitable laws that were laid down for the well-being of every part of the universe. For example, suppose that the brightness of the sun corrupts someone's eyes because they were too weak to bear such light. Obviously we should not think that the sun changed the eyes in order to satisfy some need of its own, or that it did so because it had some flaw. Nor should we blame the eyes for yielding to their master and opening to the light, even though in yielding to the light they were corrupted. So corruption is justly blamed only if it involves some flaw. Any other corruption should not be called 'corruption' at all; or at least it cannot justly be condemned, since it involves no flaw. For condemnation [*vitupera-tio*] is said to get its name from the fact that it is applicable (that is, suited or appropriate) only to a flaw [*vitio parata*].

But as I had begun to say, a flaw is bad only because it is opposed to the nature of the thing in which it is present. It is therefore obvious that the thing whose flaw we condemn has a praiseworthy nature, so much so that we must admit that our very act of condemning flaws constitutes praise of the natures whose flaws we condemn. For since the flaw is opposed to the nature, the more it destroys the integrity of the nature, the worse it is. Therefore, when you condemn a flaw, you are praising the

---

8. 1 Corinthians 3:17

thing whose integrity you miss. And to what does that integrity belong, if not to the nature? For a perfect nature is worthy of praise according to its kind; it deserves no condemnation. Therefore, if you see that something is missing from the perfection of some nature, you call it a flaw. Thus you testify that you are pleased with the nature, for in condemning its imperfection you show that you wish it were perfect.

15.   If, therefore, to condemn the flaws in those natures is to commend the beauty and dignity of the natures themselves, how much more is God, the Creator of all natures, to be praised, even in those very flaws! Natures are natures because God made them so; they are flawed to the extent that they fall away from the design of their maker; and they are condemned to the extent that the one who condemns them sees the design by which they were made, and condemns in them what he does not see in that design. And if the design by which all things were made, the highest and unchangeable wisdom of God, exists truly and in the highest degree, consider where something is heading when it falls away from that design.

But that defect would not be worthy of condemnation unless it were voluntary. For consider this: Are you right to condemn something that is as it ought to be? I think not: you should condemn only what is not as it ought to be. But no one owes[9] something that he did not receive. And to whom does he owe it, if not to the one from whom he received it? When a debt is paid back by a bequest, it is paid back to the one who made the bequest. And when a debt is paid to the lawful heirs of a creditor, it is paid to those who succeeded him by law; otherwise we would not call it a 'repayment', but a 'transfer' or 'loss' or something like that. Therefore, it is quite absurd to say that temporal things should not cease to be, for they have been placed in the order of things in such a way that they must cease to be, so that things to come can take the place of things past, so that the full beauty of times may be completely realized according to their kind. Thus temporal things do as much as was given them to do, and they

9. The Latin *debere* means both 'owe' and 'ought'. Augustine's idea in shifting between the two senses is that right conduct is a debt we owe to God, who gave us the nature that we ought to fulfill.

repay their debt to God, to whom they owe the fact that they exist in whatever degree they exist.

Anyone who grieves that these things cease to be should pay attention to his own complaint, to see if it is just and proceeds from prudence. For his very speech is woven together out of many syllables; one ceases to be, and the next takes its place. If he were so fond of one syllable of his speech that he did not want it to cease to be and give place to the rest, we would think he was completely out of his mind. So when it comes to things that pass out of existence because they were not granted existence for any longer, so that all things might be fulfilled in their own times, no one can rightly condemn this shortcoming. For no one can say, "It ought to have lasted," since it could not transgress the boundaries that had been set for it.

But in rational creatures, whether they sin or not, the beauty of the universe reaches its most suitable limit. In them either there are no sins—which is quite absurd, since (if nothing else) the one who condemns as sin what is not sin is himself sinning; or sins should not be condemned—which is no less absurd, for then people would start to praise wrongdoing, and the entire pattern of human thinking would go awry, and life would be topsy-turvy; or people would condemn something that was done as it ought to have been, which would be abominable madness, or (to put it more mildly) a most wretched error. Or else, finally, the truest thinking concludes (as indeed it does) that sins should be condemned, and that whatever is rightly condemned is condemned because it is not as it ought to be. Ask, then, what a sinful nature owes, and you will find the answer: right conduct. Ask to whom the debt is owed, and you will find the answer: God. For it is from God that it received the power to act rightly when it so willed; and it is from God that it receives misery if it does not act rightly, and happiness if it does.

No one overcomes the laws of the Almighty Creator. Every soul must pay back what it owes, either by using well what it received, or by losing what it was unwilling to use well. If it does not pay its debt by doing justice, it will pay its debt by suffering misery, for the word 'debt' applies to both of these. We could rephrase it in this way: "If it does not pay its debt by doing what it ought, it will pay its debt by suffering what it ought."

These two things are not separated by any interval of time, as if someone at one time did not do as he ought and then at some other time suffered what he ought, lest the beauty of the universe be marred, even for an instant, by having the deformity of sin without the beauty of punishment. This punishment is now hidden, but in the judgment to come it will be made manifest in the bitter anguish of unhappiness. Just as someone who is not awake is asleep, someone who does not do what he ought immediately suffers what he ought, for so great is the happiness that comes from justice that no one can fall away from it without falling into misery.

Therefore, in any defect, either the defective thing was not given anything more than it has, and so there is no blame attached—as while it exists, it should not be blamed for not existing to a higher degree, since it was not given such an existence; or else it is unwilling to have the kind of existence that it was given the power to have, if only it were willing. And since such an existence is good, the creature is guilty if it is unwilling to have it.

16.   God, on the other hand, owes nothing to anyone; he gives everything freely. Someone might say that God owes him something for his merits, but surely God did not owe him the gift of existence, since he was not around for God to owe him anything. And besides, what merit is it to turn to him from whom you have your existence, so that from him you may also have a better existence? What sort of favor are you doing him, that you can demand repayment for it? If you were unwilling to turn to him, it would not do harm to him, but to you, for you would be nothing without him, and he made you such that, unless you turn yourself toward him and pay your debt to him to whom you owe your very existence, you will not indeed be nothing, but you will certainly be wretched.

Therefore, all creatures owe something to God. First, they owe him whatever they are insofar as they are natures; and then, if they have received a will by which they can will to be better, they owe it to him to exercise this will and be what they ought to be. No one is guilty for not receiving something, but anyone who does not repay his debt to God is justly held guilty. And anyone who has received a free will and sufficient power has a debt to God.

When someone fails to do what he ought, the Creator deserves no blame; but he deserves praise when someone suffers what he ought. And in the very act of condemning someone who does not do what he ought, you are praising the one to whom he owes this debt. For if you are praised for seeing what you ought to do, although you can see it only in God, who is the unchangeable Truth, how much more should God be praised! For it was God who decreed what you ought to will, who gave you the power to will it, and who did not permit your unwillingness to go unpunished.

Now if everyone owes what he has received, and human beings were made in such a way that they necessarily sinned, then they ought to sin. Therefore, when they sin, they are doing what they ought to do. But if it is wicked to say such a thing, then no one is compelled to sin, whether by his own nature or by someone else's. For no one sins when he suffers what he does not will. If he suffers justly, he does not sin by suffering against his will; rather, he sinned by willingly doing something for which he would unwillingly suffer just punishment. And if he suffers unjustly, how does he sin? It is unjust action, not unjust suffering, that constitutes sin. So if no one is forced to sin by his own nature or by anyone else's, the only remaining possibility is that we sin by our own will.

Suppose you decide to blame sin on the Creator. You do clear the sinner, since he was simply following the decrees of his Creator; but if this line of defense succeeds, it turns out that the creature did not sin at all, and so there is nothing to blame God for. Let us therefore praise the Creator if we can defend the sinner, and let us praise him if we cannot. For if the sinner is justly defended, he is no sinner; therefore, praise the Creator. And if the sinner cannot be defended, he is a sinner insofar as he turns away from the Creator; therefore, praise the Creator. So I find no way—indeed, I feel certain that there is no way—in which God our Creator can be blamed for our sins, when I find that he deserves praise even in those very sins, not only because he punishes them, but also because they take place when someone withdraws from his truth.

EVODIUS: I am quite happy to accept what you have said, and I agree that our Creator can in no way be rightly blamed for our sins.

But I would like to know, if possible, *why* that nature did not **17.**

sin which God foreknew would not sin, and *why* that nature
sinned which God foresaw would sin. For I no longer think that
it was God's foreknowledge itself that compelled the one to sin
and the other not to sin. But if there were no cause at all, rational
creatures would not be divided into those that never sin, those
that persevere in sin, and the intermediate group of those that
sometimes sin and sometimes act rightly. What is the cause of
this division into three groups? Don't just say, "The will," because
I'm looking for the cause of the will itself. All these creatures are
of the same kind, so there must be something that causes some
of them never to will to sin, some of them always to will to sin,
and others to will it sometimes but not other times. I am certain
only that there must be some cause of this threefold will among
rational creatures, but I don't know what this cause is.

AUGUSTINE: The will is the cause of sin, but you are asking about
the cause of the will itself. Suppose that I could find this cause.
Wouldn't we then have to look for the cause of this cause? What
limit will there be on this search? Where will our questions and
discussions end?

You should not search any further than the root of the issue.
Take care that you believe in the unsurpassable truth of the saying
that the root of all evils is greed,[10] that is, willing to have more
than enough. Enough means whatever is necessary to preserve
a nature according to its kind. But greed, which in Greek is called
'philarguria',[11] does not merely have to do with the silver or coins
from which the word is derived (for it used to be that coins were
made of silver or had some silver mixed in). Rather, it should be
understood to apply to any object of immoderate desire, in any
case where someone wills to have more than enough. Such greed
is cupidity, and cupidity is a perverse will.

Therefore, a perverse will is the cause of all evils. If such a will
were in accordance with nature, it would preserve that nature
and not harm it, and so it would not be perverse. Thus we can
conclude that the root of all evils is not in accordance with nature,
and this fact gives us all we need to answer those who want to

---

10. 1 Timothy 6:10

11. That is, the love of *argurion*, which means literally 'silver' but was
commonly used in an extended sense to mean 'money'.

blame natures. But if you are asking for the cause of this root, how can it be the root of all evils? Its cause would then turn out to be the root of all evils. And as I said, once you have found that, you will have to search for *its* cause, and there will be no limit to your searching.

And besides, what could be the cause of the will before the will itself? Either it is the will itself, in which case the root of all evils is still the will, or else it is not the will, in which case there is no sin. So either the will is the first cause of sin, or no sin is the first cause of sin. And you cannot rightly assign responsibility for a sin to anyone but the sinner; therefore, you cannot rightly assign responsibility except to someone who wills it—but I don't know why you would want to look any further. Finally, whatever the cause of the will might be, it is surely either just or unjust. If it is just, someone who obeys will not sin; and if it is unjust, let him not obey it, and he will not sin.

But what if the cause of the will is violent and forces it to act **18.** against its will? Surely we are not going to repeat this over and over. Remember what we said earlier about sin and free will. But if it is too difficult to commit it all to memory, hold this brief summary in mind. Whatever the cause of the will might be, if the will cannot resist it, it is no sin to yield to it; but if the will can resist it, let it do so, and there will be no sin. What if the cause of the will deceives the will and catches it off guard? Then let the will guard against deception. What if the deception is so great that the will cannot guard against it? Then there is no sin, for who sins by doing what he cannot guard against? But there is sin, so it is possible to guard against it.

Nonetheless, even some acts committed out of ignorance are condemned and judged to be worthy of correction, as we read in Scripture. St. Paul says, "I obtained your mercy, since I acted in ignorance."[12] The Psalmist says, "Remember not the sins of my youth and of my ignorance."[13] Even things done by necessity are to be condemned, as when someone wants to act rightly but cannot. That is what the following passages mean: "I do not do the good that I will; but the evil that I hate, that I do."[14] "To will

12. 1 Timothy 1:13
13. Psalm 25:7
14. Romans 7:19

the good is present to me, but I find no way to do it."[15] "The flesh lusts against the spirit and the spirit against the flesh; for they war against each other, so that you do not do what you will."[16]

All of these troubles have come upon human beings from the sentence of death, for if they were the result of our nature and not of our penalty, they would not be sins. If we were made to act this way naturally, so that we could be no better, we would merely be acting as we ought. If human beings were good, they would be otherwise. But as it is, they are not good, and it is not in their power to be good, either because they do not see how they ought to be, or because they lack the power to be what they see they ought to be.

Who could doubt that this is a penalty? But every just penalty is a penalty for sin, and so it is also called 'punishment'. On the other hand, if this penalty (since no one doubts that it is in fact a penalty) is unjust, it is imposed by the unjust domination of some human being. But since it would be foolish to doubt the omnipotence and justice of God, this penalty is just, and it is imposed because of sin. No unjust man could secretly usurp God's dominion over human beings (as if God were unaware of what was happening) or wrest them away against his will (as if God were so weak that he could be overcome by fear or force) so as to torture them with an unjust penalty. Therefore, the only remaining possibility is that this just penalty is a consequence of the damnation of human beings.

And it is no wonder that because of our ignorance we lack the free choice of the will to choose to act rightly, or that even when we do see what is right and will to do it, we cannot do it because of the resistance of carnal habit, which develops almost naturally because of the unruliness of our mortal inheritance. It is indeed the most just penalty for sin that we should lose what we were unwilling to use well, since we could have used it well without the slightest difficulty if only we had willed to do so; thus we who knew what was right but did not do it lost the knowledge of what is right, and we who had the power but not the will to act rightly lost the power even when we have the will.

15. Romans 7:18
16. Galatians 5:17

Indeed, all sinful souls have been afflicted with these two punishments: ignorance and difficulty. Because of ignorance, error
warps our actions; because of difficulty, our lives are a torment
and an affliction. But to accept falsehoods as truths, thus erring
unwillingly; to struggle against the pain of carnal bondage and
not be able to refrain from acts of inordinate desire: these do not
belong to the nature that human beings were created with; they
are the penalty of a condemned prisoner. But when we speak of
free will to act rightly, we mean the will with which human beings
were created.

Here we come across the slanderous question that is so often **19.**
asked by those who are ready to blame their sins on anything
but themselves: "If it was Adam and Eve who sinned, what did
we poor wretches do? How do we deserve to be born in the
blindness of ignorance and the torture of difficulty? Why do we
first err in ignorance of what we ought to do, and then, when
the precepts of justice begin to be open to us and we will to do
them, we are powerless, held back by some sort of necessity of
carnal desire?"

My response is brief: let them be silent and stop murmuring
against God. Perhaps their complaint would be justified if there
were no Victor over error and inordinate desire. But in fact there
is one who is present everywhere and speaks in many ways
through the creation that serves him as Lord. He calls out to those
who have turned their backs on him and instructs those who
believe in him. He comforts the hopeful, encourages the diligent,
helps the struggling, and hears the prayers of those who cry out
to him.

You are not blamed for your unwilling ignorance, but because
you fail to ask about what you do not know. You are not blamed
because you do not bind up your own wounds, but because you
spurn the one who wants to heal you. These are your own sins.
For no one is prevented from leaving behind the disadvantage
of ignorance and seeking the advantage of knowledge, or from
humbly confessing his weakness, so that God, whose help is
effortless and unerring, will come to his assistance.

When someone acts wrongly out of ignorance, or cannot do
what he rightly wills to do, his actions are called sins because
they have their origin in that first sin, which was committed by
free will. The later sins are the just results of that first sin. Consider

this analogy. We use the word 'tongue' not only for the organ in our mouths that we move when we speak, but also for the result of this movement: namely, the form and sound of words. In this sense we say that the Greek tongue is different from the Latin tongue. In the same way, we use the word 'sin' not only for what is really sin in the strict sense, which involves actions performed knowingly and by free will, but also for the necessary result of the punishment of sin in the strict sense.

Thus we also use 'human nature' in two senses. In the strict sense, we mean the nature with which human beings were first created, a nature blameless after its kind. But we can also mean the nature of those of us who are born under the penalty of that sin: mortal, ignorant, and enslaved to the flesh. It is in this sense that St. Paul said, "For we were by nature children of wrath, even as the others."[17]

20.   But it most justly pleased God, the Governor of all things, that we who are born of that first couple should be born into ignorance, difficulty, and mortality, since our first parents fell into error, struggle, and death. In this way his justice in punishing was manifested at the birth of the human race, but in the fullness of time he showed his mercy by setting us free. For the first man did not lose his fruitfulness when he lost his happiness; and his offspring, though carnal and mortal, were able to lend a sort of beauty and dignity to the earth as things of their kind. But it was not right for his offspring to be better than he was himself. And yet if anyone was willing to turn back to God so that he might overcome the penalty that had been imposed for turning away from God, it was right for God not to hinder him, but indeed to help him. Thus the Creator showed how easily the first man could have retained the nature he was created with, since his offspring could overcome the nature they were born with.

If only one soul was created, and all human souls are descended from it, who can say that he did not sin when Adam sinned? But if souls are created individually for each new person who is born, it is not perverse—indeed, it seems altogether fitting and well-ordered—that the evil desert of the earlier soul should be part of the nature of the soul that comes later, and that the good desert

17. Ephesians 2:3

of the later soul should be part of the nature of the soul that came earlier. How would it be undeserved if the Creator willed to show that the dignity of the soul so much surpasses that of the material creation that one soul is born at the level to which another fell? For the state of that sinful soul, which fell into ignorance and difficulty, is rightly called punishment, since before its punishment the soul was better.

If another soul, not merely before it sins but at the very outset of its life, is placed under a punishment like the one that the first soul received after its blameworthy life, it has a great good for which to thank its Creator, for the merest beginning of a soul is better than the most perfect material object. For these are no mediocre goods: not only that the soul exists, which by its nature surpasses every material object; but also that it has the power to reform itself with God's help, and by pious labors to acquire all of the virtues by which it is freed from the torture of difficulty and the blindness of ignorance. If this is so, ignorance and difficulty in newborn souls are not a punishment; they are a spur to progress and a beginning of perfection.

It is no small thing to have received, before any merit of good deeds, the natural judgment by which to prefer wisdom to error and peace to difficulty, so that it might attain by diligent labor the wisdom and peace that it does not have by birth. If it refuses to do so, it is justly held guilty of sin, since it did not make good use of the ability that it was given. For although it was born into ignorance and difficulty, no necessity forces it to remain there. But it could do nothing at all if Almighty God did not create such souls. He creates the souls that do not love him and perfects the souls that love him; he offers existence to those that do not exist and happiness to those that love him.

If souls already exist somewhere in the hidden regions of God, and are sent to animate and govern the bodies of each person who is born, their duty is to rule the body, which is born of the punishment of sin, that is, of the mortality of the first man. They are to chasten the body through the virtues and subject it to a well-ordered and lawful servitude, thus preparing it for the place of heavenly incorruption where it will dwell at the opportune time, when this is in accordance with perfect order. When they first enter this life and are clothed with these mortal limbs, they necessarily forget their past life and struggle with their present life. Hence arise ignorance and difficulty, which in the first man was the punishment of mortality, a penalty of wretchedness imposed on the soul. But in the souls that came after him, this ignorance and difficulty opened the door to the duty of restoring the incorruption of the body.

These are sins only in the sense that the flesh descended from the first sinner causes ignorance and difficulty for the souls that enter it, but such "sins" are not blamed either on those souls or on their Creator. For he gave them the ability to act rightly in laborious duties, and he showed them the path of faith in the blindness of forgetfulness. But most important, he gave them the power of judgment, by which every soul knows that it should ask for knowledge where it is hindered by ignorance; that it must strive persistently in dutiful labors to conquer the difficulty of acting rightly; and that it must implore its Creator for help in its struggle.

For God, whether he speaks externally by means of the law or in the inmost chamber of the heart, decrees to every soul that it must endure this struggle. And he prepares the glory of a most blessed city for those who triumph over Satan, whose evil persuasion led the first man into wretchedness; and they take this wretchedness upon themselves in order to conquer him by their splendid faith. It is no small boast to conquer the devil by taking on the very punishment that he had boasted of inflicting on human beings when he first conquered them. But if anyone abandons this struggle because he is captured by the love of this life, he can in no way blame his disgraceful desertion on the orders of his King; instead, the Lord of all will place him under the rule of the enemy, whose shameful pay he loved so much that he deserted his own camp.

But if, instead, souls that have been created elsewhere are not sent by the Lord God, but come to inhabit bodies by their own choice, it is quite easy to see that the ignorance and difficulty that result from their own wills are in no way to be blamed on their Creator. For he is completely without fault even if he himself sends souls to dwell in bodies. In the midst of their ignorance and difficulty he leaves them the free will to ask and seek and try. He will give to those who ask, show himself to those who seek, and open to those who knock. To those who are diligent and devoted he offers the power to overcome ignorance and difficulty and receive the crown of glory. Even to those who neglect this struggle, and use their weakness as an excuse for sin, he does not impute their ignorance and difficulty as a crime. But since they prefer to remain in that state rather than make the effort to seek and to learn, to confess in humility and to pray, so that they might arrive at truth and ease, he inflicts upon them a just punishment.

There are four views about souls: (1) they come into being by **21.** propagation; (2) they are created individually for each person who is born; (3) they already exist elsewhere and are sent by God into the bodies of those who are born; (4) they sink into bodies by their own choice. It would be rash to affirm any of these. For the Catholic commentators on Scripture have not solved or shed light on this obscure and perplexing question; or if they have, I have not yet come across any such writing. What matters is that we have the faith to believe nothing false or unworthy about the nature of the Creator, for in our journey of piety we are aiming at him. If, therefore, we believe that he is something other than what he truly is, our faulty aim compels us to journey into futility and not into happiness. By contrast, if we have a false belief about a creature, we are in no danger, as long as we do not regard that belief as knowledge. We are not made happy by any creature; we are not commanded to aim at the creature but at the Creator. Accordingly, if we believe something of the Creator that is false, or is not what we ought to believe, we are deceived by a most pernicious error. For no one can achieve a happy life if he pursues something that either does not exist or cannot make him happy.

But a way has been made for us that is suited to our weakness, a way out of temporal things, so that we can contemplate the eternity of Truth and fully enjoy and cleave to it. We must believe what is past, and what is yet to come, as far as is sufficient for our journey towards eternal things. This discipline of faith is governed by divine mercy, so that it has supreme authority.

As for things present, in perceiving the changes and movements of both body and soul we recognize that all creatures are ephemeral. We can have no knowledge of these things unless we experience them. Therefore, if by divine authority we are told anything about such creatures, whether past or future, we ought to believe it without hesitation. Some of these things happened before we were able to perceive them; others will appear to our senses at some later time. Nonetheless, we ought to believe them, for they strengthen our faith and kindle our love as they remind us that God is constantly at work in history to secure our freedom.

But if any error arrogates to itself the role of divine authority, it is most forcefully refuted if it requires one to believe or affirm that there is any changeable form other than God's creation, or that there is any changeable form in the nature of God, or that the divine nature is anything more or less than the Trinity. Indeed, the pious and sober understanding of the Trinity is the focus of all Christian attention and the goal of all Christian progress. But this is not the place to discuss the unity and equality and individual properties of the persons of the Trinity. For it is easy enough— and indeed, many people have done it again and again—to call to mind the many facts about the Lord God, who creates and shapes and orders all things, that belong to a health-giving faith. Nourished by these truths, we pull ourselves up onto our feet as we begin to leave behind earthly things and set our sights on heavenly things. But to give a complete explanation of the Trinity, and to treat it in such a way that any human understanding will be forced to accept our compelling arguments (as far as is granted us in this life), is beyond the eloquence—even beyond the intelligence—of any human being. It is certainly beyond mine.

Let us therefore consider the question at hand as thoroughly as we are allowed and helped to do so. With respect to created things, we ought to believe without hesitation whatever we are told about the past or future that serves pure religion by arousing our sincerest love for God or our neighbor. When it comes to defending these beliefs against the attacks of unbelievers, either we should defend them in such a way that their unbelief is crushed under the weight of divine authority, or else we should first show that it is not foolish to believe such things, and then show that it is foolish not to believe such things. But our chief concern should be to refute false doctrine about things present, especially about unchangeable things, rather than that which concerns things in the past or future. On such matters we should try to the best of our ability to offer compelling arguments in support of our views.

Of course, in the series of temporal things, the expectation of things to come is preferable to the search into things past, since the things that Scripture tells us about the past are prefigurations or promises or testimonies of things to come. Indeed, even in the ups and downs of this life, it does not much matter how anyone used to be; all our energy is bent on what we hope to be in the future. When we are in the midst of happiness or misery, things that happened to us in the past are regarded by some sort of natural, inner sense as if they had never happened. So what does it matter to me if I do not know when I began to exist, since I know that I exist now, and I do not despair of existing in the future? There is no great harm done if I have false beliefs about the past, since the past is of no concern to me; I direct my course toward what I am going to be, guided by the mercy of my Creator.

So I must be very much on my guard against believing or thinking anything false about what I am going to be, or about Him in whose presence I am going to be, lest I leave out some necessary preparation or find myself unable to reach the goal that I have misconceived. It is just like planning what to wear. It does not matter if I have forgotten last winter, but it certainly does matter if I do not believe that there is more cold weather to come. In the same way, it does not matter if I have forgotten what might have happened to my soul long ago, as long as I pay careful attention to what I am told about preparing for the future and bear these warnings in mind.

There is no harm done to someone sailing to Rome if he has forgotten the port from which he set out, as long as he remembers where he is headed. And he is no better off for remembering his port of origin if his mistaken ideas about where Rome is cause him to run aground on the rocks. In the same way, if I do not remember the beginning of my life, it does me no harm, since I know the end in which I will rest. And it would be of no use to me to remember or speculate about the beginning of my life if I thought unworthily about God himself, the one end of all human labor, and was shipwrecked on the rocks of error.

I don't mean to imply that I forbid anyone who can to investigate what the divinely inspired Scriptures have to say about the origin of the soul, whether one soul is propagated from another, or each soul is created individually for the body that it is to animate, or God sends souls from somewhere else to govern and animate bodies, or they enter bodies of their own will. It is permissible to consider and discuss these matters if they bear on some necessary question, or if there is time to spare from more pressing matters. Rather, I said these things to keep anyone from becoming petulant when others hesitate to accept his own, perhaps better-informed, opinion on such a matter; and so that, if anyone does have a clear and certain understanding of this issue, he will not think that others have lost all hope for the future because they have no concern for the past.

22.   But however things may stand with regard to that issue, whether we should pass over it entirely or merely put off considering it until some other time, the answer to the question at hand is perfectly clear. By the perfectly upright, just, unshakable, and unchangeable majesty and substance of the Creator, souls pay the penalty for their sins, for which their own wills are alone responsible. We should look no further for the cause of sin.

But suppose that ignorance and difficulty are the natural state of the soul, that it begins there and advances toward knowledge and rest as the happy life is brought to perfection within it. Even so, the soul is not denied the power to make this progress by piety and diligent study of the highest things. If by its own will it refuses to do so, it is justly punished by being cast into deeper ignorance and greater difficulty; by the most proper and suitable government of the universe, it is placed among inferior things. The soul is not held guilty because it is naturally ignorant and powerless, but because it did not apply itself to learn and did not work to acquire ease in acting rightly.

It is natural for an infant not to know how to speak, and not to be able to do so. Such ignorance is not only blameless under the laws of grammar; it is charming and appealing to human affections. For an infant has not viciously neglected to acquire the power of speech, or viciously lost it once it had been acquired. And so if our happiness consisted in eloquence, and every lapse of grammar were taken to be as serious as a sin in the actions of life, no one would be denounced simply because his pursuit of eloquence had begun in the ignorance of infancy. But if in the perversity of his will he remained in that state, or returned to it, he would clearly deserve to be condemned. Thus even now, if ignorance of the truth and difficulty in doing right are the natural state of human beings, from which we must rise to the happiness of wisdom and rest, no one is rightly condemned for this natural beginning. But if someone refuses to go on from there, or falls back from the progress that he has made, he pays a just and well-deserved penalty.

For all these things the Creator deserves praise: for instilling in us the power to set out from such a beginning and reach the highest good; for helping us along the way; for fulfilling and completing those who make progress; and for ordaining a most just condemnation for those who sin, that is, for those who refuse to move beyond their starting point or who fall back after they make some progress. God did not create the soul evil, simply because it is not yet as great as it has the power to become; for even at its beginning it is far superior to the perfections of material objects, which any right-thinking person judges to be praiseworthy in their own way.

If the soul does not yet know what it ought to do, it is ignorant because it has not yet received such knowledge. But it *will* receive it, if only it will make good use of what it *has* received: the power to search diligently and piously if it wills to do so. And if the soul, even when it knows what to do, cannot always do it, it is powerless because it has not yet received such power. At first the higher part of the soul is enabled to perceive the goodness of an upright action, but the carnal part lags behind and is not immediately brought around to that opinion.

This very difficulty serves as a reminder that we should beseech the help of God, who is the helper of our perfection even as he is the author of our beginning. Thereby we come to cherish God more and more, for it is by his goodness and not by our own strength that we have our existence, and by his mercy that we are raised to happiness. And the more we cherish the one from whom we exist, the more firmly we will delight in him, and the more fully we will enjoy his eternity. If we cannot rightly call an ill-tended young sapling sterile, even though it waits several summers before it shows its fruitfulness, why should we not praise the Creator of the soul, who gave the soul such a beginning that by pressing forward with diligent labor it can reap the fruit of wisdom and righteousness, and who conferred upon the soul such dignity that he gave it the power to aim for happiness if it so willed?

As an objection against this way of thinking, ignorant people **23.** often bring up the death of children, and the physical pain that we often see children suffer. "Why should someone even be born," they ask, "who leaves this life before doing anything to deserve punishment or reward? How will he be treated in the future judgment? He doesn't belong with the just, since he never acted rightly; but he doesn't belong with the wicked either, since he never sinned."

The answer is this. In the vast network of the universe and of the whole creation, and in the most orderly connection of times and places, where not a leaf on a tree is created without a purpose, no human being of any kind could be superfluous. What is superfluous is to ask about the merits of someone who has not merited anything. If there can be a life that is intermediate between sin and right action, have no fear that our Judge can pronounce a sentence that is intermediate between punishment and reward.

Again, people often wonder what good it does for infants to receive the sacrament of the baptism of Christ, since baptized infants frequently die before they can know anything about their baptism. In this matter we piously and rightly believe that the faith of those who present the child to be consecrated by baptism is of benefit to the child. The wholesome authority of the Church commends this doctrine to us in order to show us how much our own faith benefits us, when it can help even those who do not yet have faith. The widow's son was not helped by his own faith, for he was dead and therefore had no faith. But because of his mother's faith he was restored to life.[18] How much more, then, can the faith of another help an infant, who cannot be blamed for any misdeeds!

But there is a stronger objection, and one that seems rather tender-hearted. People often ask about the physical torment that afflicts children who, because of their age, have not sinned (assuming that the souls by which their bodies are animated did not exist before the children themselves). "What evil did they do to deserve such suffering?"

As if there were merit in the innocence of someone who could not yet do any harm! Since God achieves some good by correcting adults through the suffering and death of children who are dear to them, why shouldn't those things take place? Once the suffering

18. Cf. Luke 7:11–15

is past, it will be for the children as if they had never suffered. And as for the adults for whose sake they suffered, either they will be better, having learned from temporal adversities to choose an upright life, or they will have no excuse to avert their punishment in the judgment to come, since they refused to let the anguish of this life turn their desire toward eternal life.

Who knows what is in store for those children, whose suffering melts the hard hearts of their elders as it cultivates their faith and tests their mercy? Who knows what reward God has prepared for them in the hidden depths of his judgments? For while it is true that they never acted rightly, they suffered without sinning. It is not without reason that the Church celebrates as martyrs the children who were killed when Herod sought the life of the Lord Jesus Christ.[19]

These slanderers, who are not serious inquirers into such questions but mere windbags, often disturb the faith of those who are less educated by bringing up the pain and suffering of animals. "What evil have animals done," they ask, "to deserve such suffering? What good can they hope for to justify such pain?"

Those who say or think such things have a completely skewed view of the world. Simply because they cannot understand the nature and grandeur of the highest good, they want everything to be as they imagine the highest good to be. They cannot think of anything better than the highest material objects, the celestial bodies, which are less subject to corruption; so they most inordinately demand that the bodies of beasts suffer neither death nor any corruption, as if they were not mortal (since they are the humblest bodies), or as if they were bad simply because celestial bodies are better.

The pain that beasts feel reveals a power that is amazing and praiseworthy in its own way, because it shows that even the souls of beasts have a strong drive toward unity in governing and animating their bodies. For what is pain but a sense of resistance to division and corruption? Thus, when the soul does not willingly or indifferently give into the physical suffering that threatens its unity and integrity, but instead faces it reluctantly and struggles against it, we see all the more clearly how eager and determined

19. Cf. Matthew 2:16

the soul is to preserve its unity. If it were not for the suffering of beasts, we would not see how great is the desire for unity in the lower animals, and so we would be less mindful than we ought to be that all things were created by the supreme, sublime, and ineffable unity of the Creator.

Indeed, if you regard them carefully and piously, every kind of creature and every movement that can be considered by the human mind speaks to us for our instruction. Their diverse movements and dispositions are like so many voices crying out to us, telling us to recognize their Creator. Of all the creatures that do not feel pleasure and pain, there is not one that does not attain the beauty of its own kind, or at least the stability of its nature, by some sort of unity. Of all those that feel the sting of pain or the allure of pleasure, there is not one that does not confess, by the very fact that it resists pain and desires pleasure, that it resists division and desires unity.

And in rational souls, the desire for knowledge (in which their nature delights) takes whatever it perceives and refers it to unity; it flees from error precisely because it resists the bewilderment of an incomprehensible ambiguity. Why else is ambiguity so troubling, if not because it has no certain unity?

Thus we see that all things, whether they offend or feel offended, whether they delight or are delighted, both quietly intimate and openly proclaim the unity of the Creator. But if the ignorance and difficulty from which we must begin this life are not natural for souls, they have been either undertaken as a duty or imposed as a punishment. And that, I think, is enough discussion on these matters.

24.   It is therefore more important to ask what the first human being was like when he was created than how his descendants were propagated. For many people think they are being quite clever by posing this question: "If the first man was created wise, why was he led astray? And if he was created foolish, why isn't God the cause of all vices, since folly is the ultimate vice?"—as if human nature were not capable of a state intermediate between wisdom and folly, a state that cannot properly be called either wisdom or folly. It is not until one is capable of either having wisdom or neglecting it that one must be called either wise or foolish. Only then is the will guilty of vicious folly. No one would be so stupid as to call an infant foolish, although it would be

even more absurd to call it wise. Therefore, an infant cannot be
called either wise or foolish, even though it is a human being;
this shows that human nature is capable of an intermediate state
that you cannot rightly call either wisdom or folly.

Thus, if someone sees a soul that is in the same state as those
who lack wisdom because of their own neglect, he would be
wrong to call it foolish, if he sees that it lacks wisdom by nature
and not because of vice. For not all ignorance of what is to be
desired and what is to be avoided counts as folly, but only vicious
ignorance. We do not call an irrational animal foolish, since it has
not received the power to be wise. Nonetheless, we often use
words improperly when there is some resemblance to the proper
meaning. For example, blindness is the greatest defect that eyes
can have; but in newborn animals it is no defect, and it is not
properly called blindness.

Therefore, if man was created in such a way that he was not
yet wise, but could receive a commandment that he was obligated
to obey, it is no surprise that he could be led astray, and it is not
unjust that he should pay the price for disobeying that commandment. Nor is his Creator the cause of vices, for it was no vice in
man that he did not yet have wisdom, since he had not yet
received the power to have it. But if he had willed to make good
use of what he already had, he could have risen to what he did
not yet have.

For it is one thing to be rational and another to be wise. By
reason one becomes capable of receiving a commandment to
which one ought to be faithful, so that one does what is commanded. The nature of reason grasps the commandment, and
obedience to the commandment brings wisdom. And just as the
nature is what grasps the commandment, the will is what obeys
the commandment. Just as the rational nature is what deserves
(so to speak) to receive the commandment, obedience to the commandment is what deserves to be rewarded with wisdom. But
the very thing by which man begins to be capable of receiving a
commandment is that by which he begins to be able to sin.

There are two ways in which one can sin before becoming wise:
either by not applying oneself to receive the commandment, or
by not obeying it once it is received. A person who is already
wise, on the other hand, sins by turning away from wisdom. For
the commandment does not come from the one who is com-

manded, but from the one who commands; and in the same way, wisdom does not come from the one who is illuminated, but from the one who illuminates.

Why, then, should we not praise the Creator of man? For man is something good, and he is better than the beasts precisely because he is capable of receiving a commandment; he is better still when he has received it, even better when he obeys it, and best of all when he is happy in the eternal light of wisdom. But sin is evil because it involves neglect: neglecting to receive the commandment, neglecting to obey it, or neglecting to persevere in the contemplation of wisdom.

Thus we see that the first man could have sinned even if he had been created wise; and since that sin would have been a matter of free choice, it would have been justly punished in accordance with divine law. The Apostle Paul says so as well: "Claiming to be wise, they were made foolish."[20] For it is pride that turns one away from wisdom, and the result of this turning away is folly. Folly is in fact a sort of blindness, as Paul says in the same passage: "And their foolish hearts were darkened."[21] What is the source of this darkness, if not their turning away from the light of wisdom? And what is the source of this turning away, if not that someone whose good is God wants to be his own good, as if he were his own God? And so it is written: "Within myself, my soul is disquieted,"[22] and "Taste it, and you will be like gods."[23]

Some people are troubled when they consider this question: "Did the first man abandon God because of his folly, or did he become foolish because he abandoned God?" If you say that he abandoned wisdom because of his folly, it will look as if he was already foolish even before he abandoned wisdom, since his folly was the cause of his abandoning wisdom. On the other hand, if you say that he became foolish because he abandoned wisdom, they will ask you whether he acted wisely or foolishly in abandoning wisdom. "If he acted wisely," they will say, "he acted rightly and therefore committed no sin. But if he acted foolishly, then

20. Romans 1:22
21. Romans 1:21
22. Psalm 42:6
23. Genesis 3:5

the folly that caused him to abandon wisdom was already in him. For only in virtue of his folly could he have acted foolishly."

This dilemma shows that the transition from wisdom to folly is made neither wisely nor foolishly, but in some intermediate way that human beings in this life can understand only by contrast with both wisdom and folly. Now no mortal becomes wise except by passing from folly to wisdom. If this transition is made foolishly, then it is not made well, which is utterly insane; and if it is made wisely, then there is wisdom in someone before he becomes wise, which is no less absurd. So we see it is made in some intermediate way that cannot properly be called either wise or foolish.

Thus, the fall of the first human being from the stronghold of wisdom to folly was neither wise nor foolish. It is much the same in sleeping and waking. To fall asleep is not the same as to be asleep, and to wake up is not the same as to be awake; rather, falling asleep and waking up are transitions from one state to the other. But there is one difference. The transitions between sleeping and waking often take place without the will, but the transitions between wisdom and folly never take place except by means of the will, and for this reason they are followed by just retribution.

Only something that is seen can incite the will to act. We control **25.** whether we accept or reject whatever we see, but we do not control what we see. Therefore, we must acknowledge that the soul as a rational substance sees both superior and inferior things; from either class it chooses what it wills, and happiness or misery follows close behind, depending on what its choice deserves. For example, in the Garden of Eden the commandment of God was seen among superior things; the suggestion of the serpent was seen among inferior things. Man had no control over what the Lord commanded or over what the serpent suggested. But that he was indeed free not to succumb to the allure of those inferior things, and was unhampered by any difficulty, because he was established in the purity of wisdom, is evident from the fact that even fools overcome those things when they are on the road to wisdom, even though they must let go of the deadly charm of destructive habits.

But here we might ask a further question. Man saw both options before him: one from the commandment of God, and the other from the suggestion of the serpent. But from what source did the devil himself receive the suggestion to desire the impiety by which he fell from heaven? If nothing he saw suggested the idea to him, he would not have done what he did; for if nothing of the sort had entered his mind, he would never have turned his attention toward wickedness. So from what source did this thing, whatever it was, enter his mind, so that he set out to do those things that made a good angel into the devil? Obviously, in order to will at all one must will *something*; and that something must either be brought to one's attention from outside through the bodily senses or enter one's mind in some obscure way.

We must therefore distinguish between two classes of things seen. One originates in the will of someone who is attempting to persuade. An example of this class is the suggestion of the devil, to which man consented when he sinned. The other class originates in the things that are present to the attention of the mind or the senses of the body. The things that are present to the attention of the mind (not including the unchangeable Trinity, which indeed is not present to the mind but far surpasses its grasp) are, first, the mind itself, by which we perceive that we are alive; and then, the body that it governs, directing each part to perform its proper activity whenever there is need of it. And any material object is present to the senses of the body.

In its contemplation of the highest wisdom—which is not the soul, since it is unchangeable—the changeable soul also looks upon itself and somehow enters its own mind. But this happens only as the soul realizes that it is not the same as God, and yet that it is something that, next to God, can be pleasing. It is better, however, if the soul simply forgets itself in the love of the unchangeable God or regards itself as worthless by comparison with him.

If instead someone takes pleasure in himself and wills to enjoy his own power in a perverse imitation of God, he becomes more and more insignificant as he desires to become greater. This is "pride, the beginning of all sin";[24] and "the beginning of pride is apostasy from God."[25] But to the pride of the devil was added a malicious envy, so that he persuaded man to the same pride for

24. Ecclesiasticus 10:13
25. Ecclesiasticus 10:12

which he knew he had been condemned. Thus man became subject to a penalty whose aim was not so much his death as his reform.

And so, just as the devil had offered himself as an example of pride, the Lord offered himself as an example of humility. Through him we have the promise of eternal life, so that, through the intercession of the blood of Christ, which was shed for us after much toil and unspeakable suffering, we may cleave to our Redeemer with such charity, and be so enraptured by his brightness, that nothing we see among inferior things will divert our gaze from superior things. And even if some such thing were brought to our attention, the everlasting damnation and torment of the devil would prevent us from desiring inferior things.

So great is the beauty of justice, so great the joy of the eternal light, that is, of the unchangeable truth and wisdom, that even if we could abide in it only one day, for the sake of that short time we would rightly and justly despise countless years of this life, full of pleasures and an abundance of transitory goods. How truly and passionately was it said that "One day in your courts is better than a thousand"![26] But one can interpret this passage in another way, by taking 'a thousand days' to refer to the mutability of time, and 'one day' to indicate the immutability of eternity.

I don't know whether I have overlooked anything in answering your questions as well as the Lord saw fit to allow me. But even if something occurs to you, the limits of this book compel us to draw to a close and rest awhile from this discussion.

26. Psalm 84:10

Reconsiderations

Book One, Chapter Nine

Near the end of his career, Augustine undertook to review all his works, establish their chronology, and reexamine them in the light of his views at the time. He called this survey *Retractationes*, from the Latin *retractare*, to rehandle or take up again. It is a mistake to call them *Retractions*, since often Augustine is perfectly satisfied with what he finds in his earlier writings. A better English title would be *Reconsiderations*.

In his *Reconsiderations* of *On Free Choice of the Will*, Augustine is chiefly concerned to distance himself from the Pelagians, a heretical group that had claimed to find support for their views in Augustine's writings on free choice.

1.　　While we were still waiting in Rome, we decided to discuss the origin of evil. We carried on the discussion in such a way that reason would raise the things that we already believed on divine authority to the level of understanding, to the extent that we could do so with God's help. And since, after careful discussion, we agreed that the sole origin of evil is the free choice of the will, the three books that grew out of that discussion were entitled *On Free Choice*. I finished Books Two and Three, as well as I could at the time, after I had been ordained a priest at Hippo Regius.

2.　　So many things were discussed in these books that quite a few issues arose that I could not elucidate, or that would have required an extended discussion. Whenever a question admitted of more than one solution, and we could not determine which of these was closest to the truth, we postponed the question with the understanding that, whatever might turn out to be the truth, we could believe, or even prove, that God ought to be praised.

We took up this discussion in order to refute those who deny that the origin of evil lies in the free choice of the will and therefore contend that we should blame evil on God, the Creator of all natures. In keeping with this perverse error, these men, the Manichees, wish to assert the existence of an unchangeable principle of evil coeternal with God. Since this was the debate we had in mind, there was no discussion in these books of the grace of God, by which he so predestines his chosen people that he himself prepares the wills of those who are already using their free choice. Consequently, wherever the subject of grace arose, it was mentioned only in passing and not given the careful treatment that would have been appropriate if it had been the principal topic of discussion. For it is one thing to search for the origin of evil and quite another to ask how we can be restored to our original innocence or press on toward a greater good.

Therefore, these new Pelagian heretics—who claim that the **3.** choice of the will is so free that they leave no room for God's grace, which they claim is given in accordance with our merits— should not congratulate themselves as if I had been pleading their cause, simply because I said many things in support of free choice that were necessary to the aim of our discussion.

Indeed, I said in Book One: "Evil deeds are punished by the justice of God." And I added, "They would not be punished justly if they were not performed voluntarily."

Again, in showing that a good will is so great a good that it is rightly preferred to all physical and external goods, I said, "Then I believe you realize that it is up to our will whether we enjoy or lack such a great and true good. For what is so much in the power of the will as the will itself?"

And in another place I said, "Then why should we hesitate to affirm that, even if we have never been wise, it is by the will that we lead and deserve a praiseworthy and happy life, or a contemptible and unhappy one?"

And again in another place I said, "From this it follows that all who will to live upright and honorable lives, if they will this more than they will transitory things, attain such a great good so easily that they have it by the very act of willing to have it."

And again elsewhere I said, "For the eternal law (to which it is time for us to return) has established with unshakable firmness that the will is rewarded with happiness or punished with unhappiness depending on its merit."

And in another place I said, "We have determined that the choice to follow and embrace one or the other lies with the will."

In Book Two I said: "For human beings as such are good things, since they can live rightly if they so will." And in another place

I said ". . . no one can act rightly except by that same free choice."

In Book Three I said, "Now we admit that this movement [sin] belongs to the will alone, and that it is voluntary and therefore blameworthy; and the only useful teaching on this topic is that which condemns and checks this movement and thus serves to rescue our wills from their fall into temporal goods and turn them toward the enjoyment of the eternal good. Therefore, what need is there to ask about the source of the movement by which the will turns away from the unchangeable good toward changeable good?"

And in another place I said, "How clearly the truth speaks through you! You could not help thinking that the only thing that is within our power is that which we do when we will it. Therefore, nothing is so much within our power as the will itself, for it is near at hand the very moment that we will."

Again, in another place I said, "For if you are praised for seeing what you ought to do, although you can see it only in God, who is the unchangeable Truth, how much more should God be praised! For it was God who decreed what you ought to will, who gave you the power to will it, and who did not permit your unwillingness to go unpunished." And then I added, "Now if everyone owes what he has received, and human beings were made in such a way that they necessarily sinned, then they ought to sin. Therefore, when they sin, they are doing what they ought to do. But if it is wicked to say such a thing, then no one is compelled to sin, whether by his own nature or by someone else's."

And furthermore I said, "And besides, what could be the cause of the will before the will itself? Either it is the will itself, in which case the root of all evils is still the will, or else it is not the will, in which case there is no sin. So either the will is the first cause of sin, or no sin is the first cause of sin. And you cannot rightly assign responsibility for a sin to anyone but the sinner; therefore, you cannot rightly assign responsibility except to someone who wills it."

And a little further on I said, "For who sins by doing what he cannot guard against? But there is sin, so it is possible to guard against it." Pelagius made use of this statement in some book of his; when I responded to his book I decided to call my own book *On Nature and Grace.*

In these and similar passages I did not mention the grace of **4.**
God, which was not then under discussion. Consequently, the
Pelagians think, or could think, that I held their view. Far from
it. As I emphasized in these passages, it is indeed by the will that
we sin or live rightly. But unless the will is liberated by grace
from its bondage to sin and is helped to overcome its vices, mortals
cannot lead pious and righteous lives. And unless the divine grace
by which the will is freed preceded the act of the will, it would
not be grace at all. It would be given in accordance with the will's
merits, whereas grace is given freely. I have dealt satisfactorily
with these questions in other works, refuting these upstart heretics
who are the enemies of grace. But even in *On Free Choice of the
Will*, which was not aimed at the Pelagians (who did not yet exist)
but at the Manichees, I was not completely silent on the subject
of grace, which the Pelagians in their abominable impiety are
trying to take away altogether.

Indeed, I said in Book Two, "But you must remember that even
the lowest goods can exist only from him from whom all good
things come, that is, from God." And a little further on I said,
"Thus, the virtues, by which one lives rightly, are great goods;
the beauty of various material objects, without which one can
live rightly, are the lowest goods; and the powers of the soul,
without which one cannot live rightly, are intermediate goods.
No one uses the virtues wrongly, but the other goods, both the
lowest and the intermediate, can be used either rightly or wrongly.
The virtues cannot be used wrongly precisely because it is their
function to make the right use of things that can also be used
wrongly, and no one uses something wrongly by using it rightly.
So the adundant generosity of the goodness of God has bestowed
not only the great goods, but also the lowest and intermediate
goods. His goodness deserves more praise for the great goods
than for the intermediate goods, and more for the intermediate
goods than for the lowest goods; but it deserves more praise for
creating all of them than it would deserve for creating only some
of them."

And in another place I said, "You must simply hold with
unshaken faith that every good thing that you perceive or understand or in any way know is from God."

And again in another place I said, "But since we cannot pick
ourselves up voluntarily as we fell voluntarily, let us hold with

confident faith the right hand of God—that is, our Lord Jesus Christ—which has been held out to us from on high."

5.   And in Book Three, in making the statement that, as I have already mentioned, Pelagius himself quoted from my works ("For who sins by doing what he cannot guard against? But there is sin, so it is possible to guard against it."), I immediately went on to say, "Nonetheless, even some acts committed out of ignorance are condemned and judged to be worthy of correction, as we read in Scripture. St. Paul says, 'I obtained your mercy, since I acted in ignorance.' The Psalmist says, 'Remember not the sins of my youth and of my ignorance.' Even things done by necessity are to be condemned, as when someone wants to act rightly but cannot. That is what the following passages mean. . . . 'To will the good is present to me, but I find no way to do it.' 'The flesh lusts against the spirit and the spirit against the flesh; for they war against each other, so that you do not do what you will.' All of these troubles have come upon human beings from the sentence of death, for if they were the result of our nature and not of our penalty, they would not be sins. If we were made to act this way naturally, so that we could do no better, we would merely be acting as we ought. If human beings were good, they would be otherwise. But as it is, they are not good, and it is not in their power to be good, either because they do not see how they ought to be, or because they lack the power to be what they see they ought to be. Who could doubt that this is a penalty? But every just penalty is a penalty for sin, and so it is called 'punishment'. On the other hand, if this penalty (since no one doubts that it is in fact a penalty) is unjust, it is imposed by the unjust domination of some human being. But since it would be foolish to doubt the omnipotence and justice of God, this penalty is just, and it is imposed because of sin. No unjust man could secretly usurp God's dominion (as if God were unaware of what was happening) or wrest them away against his will (as if God were so weak that he could be overcome by fear or force) so as to torture them with an unjust penalty. Therefore, the only remaining possibility is that this just penalty is a consequence of the damnation of human beings."

And again in another place I say, "But to accept falsehoods as truths, thus erring unwillingly; to struggle against the pain of carnal bondage and not be able to refrain from acts of inordinate desire: these do not belong to the nature that human beings were created with; they are the penalty of a condemned prisoner. But when we speak of free will to act rightly, we mean the will with which human beings were created."

Thus, long before the Pelagian heresy had arisen, I argued just **6.** as if I were combatting the Pelagians. For when it is said that all good things—the great, the intermediate, and the lowest goods— come from God, free choice of the will is among the intermediate goods, because it can be used either rightly or wrongly, but we cannot live rightly without it. The right use of free choice is virtue, which is found among the great goods, which no one can use wrongly. And since, as I have said, all good things—the great, the intermediate, and the lowest goods—are from God, it follows that the right use of our free will, which is virtue and is included among the great goods, is also from God.

Then I said that the grace of God frees us from the misery that was justly imposed upon sinners. For human beings cannot pick themselves up voluntarily—that is, by their own free choice—as they fell voluntarily. To the misery imposed by this just condemnation belong ignorance and difficulty, which afflict all human beings from the very outset of their lives. And no one is freed from that evil except by the grace of God. The Pelagians deny that this misery derives from a just condemnation, for they disbelieve in original sin. But as I argued in Book Three, even if ignorance and difficulty belonged to the nature with which human beings were originally created, God would still deserve praise and not blame.

This discussion was directed against the Manichees, who do not accept the Old Testament, where the story of the original sin is told. And they have the reprehensible impudence to claim that whatever they read on that subject in the letters of the apostles was inserted later by those who corrupted the text of Scripture, and was not written by the apostles at all. In arguing against the Pelagians, on the other hand, we must defend our views from the Old as well as the New Testament, since they claim to accept both.

This book begins: "Please tell me: isn't God the cause of evil?"